THE AUDITOR'S
REPORTING OBLIGATION

1

THE AUDITOR'S REPORTING OBLIGATION

THE MEANING AND IMPLEMENTATION OF THE FOURTH STANDARD OF REPORTING

By D. R. Carmichael, CPA, Ph.D.
Assistant Director,
Auditing and Reporting Division
American Institute of
Certified Public Accountants

Published by the
American Institute of
Certified Public Accountants, Inc.
666 Fifth Avenue,
New York, N.Y. 10019

The project advisory committee
for this Auditing Research Monograph
was composed of:

Harry T. Magill, *Chairman*
Richard A. Nest
William H. Conkling
Richard D. Fitzgerald
Walter G. Kell
John D. Harrington

Preface

This first auditing research monograph is evidence of the Institute's commitment to engage in auditing research.

The function of auditing is the solid base on which the entire public accounting profession rests. Without the audit function, there would be no public practice by the profession.

Long ago the Institute concluded that standards were needed to provide guidelines for auditors in performing their function. The Institute's Committee on Auditing Procedure responded to this need by issuing statements (now numbering over fifty) on procedure and related matters. Most of these statements were issued without benefit of in-depth research, although research would undoubtedly have been helpful.

Despite the importance of the audit function and the need for guidelines in performing it, auditing research has received little attention in comparison with that devoted to accounting research. About three years ago, the Institute set out to correct this imbalance by engaging Douglas R. Carmichael as an auditing research consultant.

Since then ten statements on auditing procedure have been issued—far more than in any other three-year period in the history of the committee. The presence of an audit research capability was a significant factor in attaining this productivity in that many research papers were provided to the committee with respect to subjects on their agenda.

The greater depth of research which will almost certainly be stimulated by this monograph series should further improve the quality of committee pronouncements. The result, in my opinion, will represent a highly valuable contribution to the accounting profession.

LEONARD M. SAVOIE
Former Executive Vice-President
American Institute of Certified Public Accountants

Table of Contents

1

The Philosophy of the Fourth Reporting Standard and Problems of Implementation

In 1947 the Institute's Committee on Auditing Procedure proposed nine tentative generally accepted auditing standards as measures of the quality of independent audits.[1] Three of these standards were concerned with the independent auditor's report. When the auditing standards were issued in final form, a fourth standard had been added to the reporting standards.[2]

The fourth standard of reporting places an important reporting obligation on the auditor.

> The report shall either contain an expression of opinion regarding the financial statements taken as a whole, or an assertion to the effect that an opinion cannot be expressed. When an over-all opinion cannot be expressed, the reasons therefor should be stated. In all cases where an auditor's name is associated with financial statements the report should contain a clear-cut indication of the character of the auditor's examination, if any, and the degree of responsibility he is taking.

The objective of this standard is to enable shareholders, credit grantors, and others who use financial statements to determine the extent to which financial statements reported on by CPAs may be relied upon. In compliance with the fourth standard of reporting, a CPA who allows his name to be associated with financial statements

---

[1] Committee on Auditing Procedure, "Tentative Statement of Auditing Standards—Their Generally Accepted Significance and Scope," American Institute of Accountants, New York, 1947.
[2] Committee on Auditing Procedure, "Generally Accepted Auditing Standards—Their Significance and Scope," American Institute of Accountants, New York, 1954.

must clearly indicate the degree of responsibility he is taking with respect to the statements.

Rationale of the Standard

Another way of looking at the fourth reporting standard is that it requires the auditor to be as concerned with the fair presentation of his report as he is with the fair presentation of the financial statements of the company reported upon. The auditor's responsibility in this regard is twofold: "The report should contain (1) a clear-cut indication of the character of the examination, if any, and (2) the degree of responsibility he is taking." In other words, the auditor's report should not mislead financial statement users as to either the extent of the examination or the responsibility assumed in expressing his opinion.

Implicit in the fourth standard of reporting is the notion that an auditor may assume different degrees of responsibility for a set of financial statements. A corollary of this notion is that there are *degrees of qualification* which the auditor may apply to his opinion on financial statements. A consequence of this possibility of qualifying an opinion in different degrees is that audit opinions may be *ranked* according to the amount of responsibility assumed.

All possible types of audit reports ranked in accordance with the degree of responsibility assumed result in a set of *graded* opinions. Others have identified the role of graded opinions in the decision process of financial statement users:

> Given the existence of a set of graded opinions one must ask the question: Do the different grades have any impact on the allocation of resources? The assumption is implicitly made that at least the learned statement user can distinguish between the different grades.[3]

Presumably, more credibility attaches to financial statements in relation to the extent of responsibility assumed by the reporting auditor. Accordingly, a financial statement user, in making his resource allocation decision, places less reliance on the financial statements in correspondence to the degree to which the audit report is qualified. Thus, the audit profession fills a social need by reporting on the reliability of financial information.

Society, however, needs dependable, reliable financial information. Some would argue that when the responsibility of the auditor for the reliability of the information is qualified to some degree, the report

---

[3]H. M. Anderson, J. W. Giese, Jon Booker, "Some Propositions About Auditing," *The Accounting Review*, July 1970, p. 525.

2

does not fulfill the social need. Naturally, the responsibility for evaluating how much reliability is lost by the auditor's qualification should not rest with the users of audited financial statements. The intention of the fourth reporting standard is to place on the auditor, rather than the reader of his report, the responsibility for evaluating and reporting upon the adequacy of his examination and the responsibility assumed for the reliability of the financial statements. However, carried to the extreme, the responsibility placed on the auditor would be to decide that financial information was either reliable or not reliable. If the information were reliable he would issue his report; if it were unreliable he would not be associated with the information. Since this clear-cut dichotomy is not feasible, given the inherent limitations of financial statement preparation and audit examination, the accounting profession has adopted the position of limiting the degrees of qualification that may be applied to audit opinions.

The degree of responsibility which an auditor may assume for the reliability of financial information through his audit report is divided into four basic types, each of which is characterized by an audit report that may be issued in conjunction with audited financial statements. As explained in Chapter 10 of Statement on Auditing Procedure (SAP) No. 33, these types are as follows:

Unqualified Opinion

8. An unqualified opinion that financial statements present fairly financial position and results of operations may be expressed only when the independent auditor has formed the opinion, on the basis of an examination made in accordance with generally accepted auditing standards, that the presentation conforms with generally accepted accounting principles applied on a consistent basis and includes all informative disclosures necessary to make the statements not misleading.

Qualified Opinion

9. When a qualified opinion is intended by the independent auditor, the opinion paragraph of the standard short-form report should be modified in a way that makes clear the nature of the qualification. It should refer specifically to the subject of the qualification and should give a clear explanation of the reasons for the qualification and of the effect on financial position and results of operations, if reasonably determinable. Reference in the opinion paragraph to a note to the financial statements or to a preceding paragraph in the report that describes the circumstances is an acceptable method of clarifying the nature of a qualification. However, a qualification based upon the scope of the examination ordinarily should be covered entirely in the independent auditor's report. When a qualification is so material as to negative an expression of opinion as to the fairness of the financial statements as a whole, either a disclaimer of opinion or an adverse opinion is required.

Adverse Opinion

12. An adverse opinion is an opinion that the financial statements *do not* present fairly the financial position or results of operations in conformity with generally accepted accounting principles.

13. An adverse opinion is required in any report where the exceptions as to fairness of presentation are so material that in the independent auditor's judgment a qualified opinion is not justified.

Disclaimer of Opinion

14. When he has not obtained sufficient competent evidential matter to form an opinion on the fairness of presentation of the financial statements as a whole, the independent auditor should state in his report that he is unable to express an opinion on such statements. The necessity of disclaiming an opinion may arise either from a serious limitation on the scope of examination or from the existence of unusual uncertainties concerning the amount of an item or the outcome of a matter materially affecting financial position or results of operations, causing the independent auditor not to be able to form an opinion on the financial statements as a whole.

Scrutiny of these report categories leads to the conclusion that while an unqualified opinion, a disclaimer of opinion, and an adverse opinion are defined, the qualified opinion category is not specifically defined. All subjects of qualification which lead either to an adverse opinion or a disclaimer of opinion if they are not "so material as to negate an expression of opinion" would lead to a qualified opinion. Chapter 10 of SAP No. 33 explains the circumstances leading to the various types of reports and gives numerous examples of the language and form to be used when they are issued, but does little to distinguish between qualified opinions and the more extreme types of reports. This monograph expands on the factors to be considered in the reporting decision and explains the criteria that determine "when a qualification is so material as to negate an expression of opinion."

As used in this monograph, "report" means the written communication by the auditor concerning the nature and conclusions of his professional examination. "Opinion" is too limited for this purpose since, technically, only the auditor's conclusions are expressed in his *opinion* and the term does not include the description of the examination. In addition, a disclaimer of opinion is a report with a conclusion that no opinion can be expressed; consequently, a disclaimer cannot be referred to as an opinion. Historically, "report," "opinion," and "certificate" have been used interchangeably to mean report, as defined in this monograph. In the early 1900s many auditors' reports contained the phrase "we hereby certify" and the report was referred to as a certificate. By the mid-1930s the term "certificate" had been abandoned in connection with audit reports because it implied an unwarranted degree of exactitude. However, the term was incorporated into the Securities Act of 1933 and SEC regulations, which—unfortunately—perpetuated its use.

Problems of Implementation

The basic guideline for implementing the fourth reporting standard is set forth in paragraph 9 of Chapter 10 of SAP No. 33.

> When a qualification is so material as to negative an expression of opinion as to the fairness of the financial statements as a whole, either a disclaimer of opinion or an adverse opinion is required.

Using this criterion, an auditor must (1) distinguish between a "subject to" qualified opinion and disclaimer of opinion when financial statements are affected by a material uncertainty, (2) distinguish between an "except for" qualified opinion and an adverse opinion when there has been a departure from generally accepted accounting principles, and (3) distinguish between an "except for" qualification and a disclaimer of opinion when audit scope has been restricted. However, auditors differ concerning the dividing line between "material enough to warrant qualification" and "sufficiently material to negate an overall opinion."

The main purpose of this monograph is to report and evaluate the criteria actually used by auditors in deciding whether an opinion should be qualified or disclaimed when there is a major uncertainty, or qualified or adverse when there is a serious departure from generally accepted accounting principles. For reasons explained in the next chapter on the evolution of the fourth reporting standard, problems of scope limitation and the appraisal of the sufficiency of an examination for expressing an opinion are not of central concern in this monograph.

Comments made to the AICPA by the SEC, stock exchanges, and individual auditors as well as investors have indicated primary concern with the problem of evaluating major uncertainties—situations in which neither the auditor, the company's management, nor anyone else can predict the outcome of an event. Such matters should always be disclosed in financial statements. After disclosure, however, the question remains of whether the opinion should be qualified "subject to" the effect of the uncertainty on the financial statements or whether a more extreme indication of the uncertainty is necessary. Consequently, the role of major uncertainties in the reporting decision receives extensive treatment in this monograph.

The uncertainty problem also raises the question of the need for an adverse opinion in certain situations. If there is uncertainty concerning the realizability of an asset, for example, and a careful appraisal indicates limited prospects for recovery, failure to make an adjustment of undeterminable size could support a contention that the statements are not fairly presented in conformity with generally accepted accounting principles. Accordingly, this monograph also considers the criteria for distinguishing between an adverse opinion and a disclaimer of opinion.

Comments to the Institute have also indicated a concern with another problem related to uncertainties—the proliferation of "subject to" qualifications. A portion of this concern is attributable to the problem of distinguishing uncertainties requiring qualification from those requiring a disclaimer of opinion. In addition, concern exists over substitution of the "subject to" form of qualification in situations that might be more appropriately described by an "except for" qualification. Consequently, distinguishing between "except for" and "subject to" qualifications is also a problem of interest in this monograph.

The consistency exception is one type of opinion qualification that is fairly common but which is excluded from consideration in this monograph. In contrast to the other forms of report modification, consistency exceptions have received a fair amount of attention from other researchers. In addition, application of the consistency standard per se does not usually lead to questions involving exceptions sufficiently material to negate an overall opinion. Unless the accounting change is to a principle or practice which lacks general acceptance, an evaluation of whether the change is sufficiently material to require an adverse opinion is not ordinarily necessary.

In summary, this monograph is devoted to a study of the following problems which arise in implementing the fourth standard of reporting:

1. The distinction between qualified opinions on the one hand and disclaimers of opinion and adverse opinions on the other.
2. The distinction between a disclaimer of opinion and an adverse opinion.
3. The appropriate use of the "subject to" form of qualification.

Research Method

Since auditors currently issue reports with other-than-unqualified opinions with only the limited criteria of formal pronouncements as a guide, they must—at least in their own minds—use additional criteria which have not been codified. The first step in this research project was to attempt to determine what criteria are actually used by auditors in deciding what type of audit report to issue.

Critical analysis of individual cases seemed the most promising form of inquiry for reaching valid conclusions concerning reporting criteria. A judgment sample seemed necessary since not all reports

6

containing other than unqualified opinions were of interest. Of greatest interest were reports that brought the evaluation of reporting criteria into focus. For example, an opinion qualified subject to a particular uncertainty which in the next year became a disclaimer based on the same uncertainty represents the type of report that highlights criteria for the distinction between an exception material enough to qualify an opinion, but not sufficiently material to negate an overall opinion. Any reporting problem in which alternative types of reports were considered also brings reporting criteria into focus. Not all of these situations, however, were readily apparent when reviewing published financial statements. Consequently, the cooperation of auditors was sought in securing information on reporting criteria on an individual case basis.

Fortunately, there are factors which operate to make reliable information on the reporting decision available *within* a firm. The decision to disclaim an opinion or express an adverse opinion is a major step not to be taken capriciously. Opinion qualifications are serious matters; consequently, rather comprehensive documentation of the decision process often exists. Frequently, the partner in charge of the engagement seeks the counsel of a fellow partner—in which case memos may exist—or he corresponds with technical experts in the executive office of his firm. In addition, letters are sometimes prepared to explain the reason for the other-than-unqualified opinion to the client's management—who naturally desire clarification of such matters.

Several public accounting firms cooperated in making pertinent files on audit reports available for review. Over 2,000 reports were read, and over 300 cases were reviewed in depth. In some instances, promising reporting situations were identified for which documentation of the sort described did not exist. Memoranda were prepared for these situations in response to requests for information on the reporting decision. Although post-justification of the report decision could be criticized on the grounds that more and different reasons might be offered than actually influenced the decision, substantial agreement existed between the reporting criteria explained in both the pre-report data and the post-report data.

Determination of reporting criteria based on factual information of how auditors actually decide what type of report is appropriate may be characterized as an inductive research method. However, the factual information is very specific to the decision context, and the development of general reporting criteria required concurrent formulation of a conceptual classification scheme to allow sufficient generalization. No useful theoretical scheme for classifying the factual information existed. For example, the single existing criterion for determining whether a "subject to" qualification or a disclaimer of opinion was appropriate could be stated quite succinctly—when the uncertainty was sufficiently material. Consequently, development of reporting criteria required a continual balancing of inductive and deductive methods. This continual interplay of methods was also necessitated by a desire to develop reporting criteria which were not only more specific than the criteria found in existing pronouncements but also normative, that is, the criteria that should be used.

As a pattern developed from the process of reviewing audit reports and related memoranda, the emerging scheme of reporting criteria was compared in open-ended interviews with the views of several auditors regarded as experts on the subject of reporting within their own firms. These interviews were not a major source of evidence, but served primarily to test the reasonableness of the developing criteria.

Although library research alone was obviously insufficient for the task of achieving a practicable solution to the problem of developing reporting criteria, it was also obvious that library research and the related application of the deductive method was necessary and could not be omitted if some aspects of the problem were to be covered adequately.

An understanding of the emergence and historical development of the attitude expressed in the fourth standard of reporting seemed essential. The steps leading up to the present standard, the forces that caused them, and their responsiveness to these forces all have a bearing on any attempt to develop better guidelines for implementation of the fourth standard. In addition to serving as a review of the literature, tracing the historical development of reporting criteria explains the foundation on which we must build and identifies the underlying assumptions of the present criteria. If any of these assumptions are no longer valid, they must be replaced.

When an auditor's responsibility is raised as an issue in a court of law, the representations in the audit report are a logical starting point for determining liability. The literature concerning an auditor's responsibility is constructed around the language of the standard short-form report and, in a sense, the auditor's responsibilities are all contained within his report. Legal responsibility for the validity and understandability of his representations is an inescapable part of the environment in which an auditor expresses his opinion on the reliability of financial statements. Since departures from the standard short-form report are intended to modify the usual responsibilities assumed when the standard short-form report is issued, an exploration of the legal liability aspects of report modification seemed essential.

Relation to Auditing Theory and Practice

The relationship of this monograph to auditing theory and practice in general deserves some attention.

In *The Philosophy of Auditing*, Mautz and Sharaf explain five major, or primary, concepts of auditing theory: evidence, due audit care, fair presentation, independence, and ethical conduct.[4] The concept of fair presentation is further subdivided into three subconcepts—accounting propriety, adequate disclosure, and audit obligation. They describe audit obligation as the auditor's responsibility for the fair presentation of his own report and effectively equate this obligation with the fourth standard of reporting.

This monograph is, therefore, an empirical extension of the concept of audit obligation identified by Mautz and Sharaf in their outline of auditing theory.

The relationship of this monograph to practice may seem obvious; the basic subject matter of the monograph—the decision of what type of audit report to issue—is considered in every audit engagement. However, this perception of the relationship focuses on the problems of practice at the practitioner level. Although the content of the monograph may, and I hope will, be of use to auditors in their daily practice, the primary relationship of the monograph to practice is at the profession level—those problems which face the profession collectively rather than the problems raised in each individual audit.

Summary

The fourth standard of reporting requires the auditor to prepare his report in a manner which clearly indicates to financial statement users the degree of reliance which may be placed on the statements. This basic indication of reliability is accomplished by identifying the report as one of four possible types: (1) an unqualified opinion, (2) a qualified opinion, (3) an adverse opinion, or (4) a disclaimer of opinion. Within these categories further refinements are possible, but need not concern us at this point.

This monograph is directed to resolving three major problems which arise in the implementation of the fourth reporting standard. First, the distinction between qualified opinions on the one hand and disclaimers of opinion and adverse opinions on the other presently rests on vague criteria which require elaboration. Second, in some cases of major uncertainty, an adverse opinion may be more appropriate than a disclaimer of opinion, and criteria for this type of situation require refinement. Finally, in some situations in which the "subject to" form of qualified opinion is presently issued, another more explicit, or descriptive, form of qualification may more adequately describe the situation.

---

[4] R. K. Mautz and Hussein A. Sharaf, *The Philosophy of Auditing*, American Accounting Association, 1961. Chapter 7 discusses fair presentation.

The research method employed was a combination of inductive and deductive methods. Chapters 2 and 3 are based on library research, while Chapters 4 through 7 are based on a combination of methods. Chapter 2 traces the evolution of report categories in professional literature. Chapter 3 analyzes legal cases which have dealt with other than unqualified opinions. Chapter 4 presents an overview of the central reporting concepts derived from a study of audit reports and supporting documentation. Chapters 5, 6, and 7 deal specifically with the major reporting problems. Finally, Chapter 8 summarizes the conclusions and offers the author's recommendations concerning all three of the reporting problems. An appendix explores the interrelationships of auditing theory, practice, and research.

This monograph is written for the professional accountant, or individuals with equivalent technical knowledge. The discussion begins at a level which presumes a general familiarity with the technical language of the profession.

Extensive use is made of factual cases to illustrate abstract concepts. Since the cases were obtained on a confidential basis, the names, dates, and amounts have been changed. However, in all cases the relative relationships of the amounts involved have been retained. Some readers may wish to facilitate reading of the monograph by not reading all cases. Reading a case should be considered essential only if the reader feels it is required to gain a fuller understanding of the general discussion of a reporting concept.

2

Evolution of Report Categories

This chapter traces the development of distinct classes of audit reports which allow the knowledgeable report reader to characterize a given audit report as being, for example, either a qualified opinion or a disclaimer of opinion. The purposes of this discussion are to place present practice in context, indicate the influence of past events on the positions adopted in professional literature, and suggest the next step in the evolution of reporting standards.

Milestones in Report Differentiation

The evolution of distinct types of reports can be traced through the literature on accountants' reports issued by the Institute. Reports originate in practice as the result of an informed practitioner attempting to convey concisely the results of an audit. A useful and effective solution to a difficult reporting situation is noticed by practitioners and perpetuated in their own practice by adaptation to analogous situations. Eventually a practice is codified in the literature of the professional association.

A "Standard" Short-Form Report. In 1934, a form of audit report was recommended for the first time as a "standard" form as a result of the Institute's correspondence with the New York Stock Exchange in the years 1932 to 1934. Recommendation of a "standard" form was a necessary first step in the development of distinct types of reports. Any deviation from the standard language would put the informed reader "on notice." Without standard wording, a reader would have difficulty assessing the significance of the words chosen. Although prior Institute pronouncements had contained recommended reports, they were not considered "standard" wording. The correspondence with the New York Stock Exchange marked a whole new approach to reporting.

Prior to use of the recommended form, a distinction was drawn between long and short "certificates." The long certificate should not be confused with a long-form report. SAP No. 33 (Chapter 12, paragraph 1) contrasts a long-form report with a short-form report, as follows:

> In addition to the basic financial statements these reports ordinarily include details of the items in these statements, statistical data, explanatory comments, other informative material, some of which may be of a nonaccounting nature, and sometimes a description of the scope of the auditor's examination more detailed than the description in the usual short-form reports.

An early auditing textbook contrasts the short certificate with the long certificate as follows:

> The "long" or descriptive certificate, in addition to certifying to the accuracy of accounts, states briefly the main verification work done to determine that the statements presented are true and correct.[1]

Some descriptive reports dealt with the accounting policies of the company as well as with audit procedures followed. Consequently, distinguishing a "qualified" certificate from a "descriptive" certificate was not a simple task even though the distinction between a "qualified" and an "unqualified" certificate was generally understood among public accountants. (See Figures 2-1 to 2-3, pages 13 to 15.) As early as 1915 an article by George O. May explained the form and character of qualifications.[2]

Since the choice between a short and a descriptive certificate was unrestricted, an average report reader might have had difficulty in identifying a qualified certificate. The recommendation of a standard form of report was a necessary step forward in distinguishing types of reports, but the descriptive certificate did not immediately disappear from practice.

Withheld Opinion. With the issuance in 1939 of SAP No. 1, "Extensions of Auditing Procedure," a new distinction was introduced in types of reports. Prior to that time some reports included a description of what the auditor had done and what he had not done, without an unequivocal statement of what responsibility the auditor took for the financial statements. Although procedures were recited in considerable detail, the final expression of opinion was introduced by

---

[1] J. Hugh Jackson, *Auditing Problems,* The Ronald Press Company, New York, 1929, p.362.

[2] George O. May, "Qualifications in Certificates," *The Journal of Accountancy,* October 1915, pp. 248-259.

Figure 2-1   A Descriptive Certificate—Unqualified

CERTIFICATE OF ACCOUNTANTS

New York, February 6, 1924

To the Stockholders of the
American Locomotive Company:

We have examined the books of the American Locomotive Company and its subsidiary companies, the Montreal Locomotive Works, Limited, and the American Locomotive Sales Corporation, for the year ending December 31, 1923, and find that the accompanying consolidated balance sheet at that date and the relative income account are correctly prepared therefrom.

The charges during the period to property account and to reserve for additions and betterments represent only actual additions and sufficient provision has been made for accruing renewals and depreciation.

The valuations of the stocks on hand, as shown by inventory certified by responsible officials, have been carefully made at prices not in excess of cost or market and due allowance has been made for old or inactive stocks. Full provision has been made for bad and doubtful accounts and bills receivable and for all ascertainable liabilities. We have verified the cash and securities by actual inspection or by certificates from the depositaries, and

WE CERTIFY that, in our opinion, the balance sheet is properly drawn up so as to show the financial position of the American Locomotive Company and its subsidiary companies at December 31, 1923, and the relative income account is a fair and correct statement of the net earnings for the fiscal year ending at that date.

Price, Waterhouse & Co.

---

wording such as "subject to the foregoing." If the report contained numerous limiting expressions or comments, as was common in descriptive reports, even the informed reader would have difficulty in determining the meaning of the report.

To eliminate this practice, SAP No. 1 contained the following much-quoted paragraph:

> The independent certified public accountant should not express the opinion that financial statements present fairly the position of the company and the results of its operations, in conformity with generally accepted accounting principles, when his exceptions are such as to negative the opinion, or when the examination has been less in scope than he considers necessary. In such circumstances, the independent certified public accountant should limit

13

40 Exchange Place, New York
March 15, 1924

To the Board of Directors of the
General Electric Company
120 Broadway, New York.

Dear Sirs:

We have examined the books and accounts of the General Electric Company for the year ended December 31, 1923, and hereby certify that the Condensed Profit and Loss account and Balance Sheet appearing on pages 13-15 of this report are in accordance with the books and, in our opinion, correctly record the results of the operations of the Company for the year and the condition of its affairs as at December 31, 1923.

We have verified the cash and securities by actual count and inspection or by certificates which we have obtained from the depositaries. The valuations at which the investment securities are carried have been approved by a Committee of the Board of Directors and, in our opinion, are conservative. Our audit has not included the examination of the accounts of certain of the companies which are controlled through stock ownership, but Balance Sheets of these companies have been submitted to us.

We have scrutinized the notes and accounts receivable and are satisfied that full provision has been made for possible losses through bad and doubtful debts.

Certified inventories of merchandise, work in progress, and materials and supplies have been submitted to us and we have satisfied ourselves that these inventories have been taken in a careful manner, that full allowance has been made for old or inactive stocks, and that they are conservatively stated on the basis of cost or market, whichever is lower. Provision has also been made for possible allowances or additional expenditures on completed contracts.

Expenditures capitalized in the property and plant accounts during the year were properly so chargeable as representing additions or improvements. Ample provision has been made in the operating accounts for repairs, renewals and depreciation, and also liberal reserves for contingencies.

Yours truly,

Marwick, Mitchell & Co.

his report to a statement of his findings and, if appropriate, his reasons for omitting an expression of opinion.

This paragraph may be viewed as the historical foundation of the present position which distinguishes several distinct types of audit reports. However, the primary thrust of SAP No.1 was to make the audit procedures of inventory observation and receivable confirmation generally accepted. In other words, the statement was concerned primarily with the adequacy of the examination. Public accountants were reminded of their responsibility with respect to the scope of the examination as follows:

> It is the responsibility of the accountant—and one which he cannot escape—to determine the scope of the examination which he should make before giving his opinion on the statements under review.

After issuing SAP No. 1, the Committee on Auditing Procedure interpreted the influence of the omission of the extended or other important procedures on the expression of an opinion in several statements, three of which (SAP Nos. 2, 11, and 13) were entitled "The Auditor's Opinion on the Basis of a Restricted Examination." Another statement (SAP No. 8) dealt with the auditor's report on interim financial statements. In SAP No. 8, the Committee on Auditing

Figure 2-3   A Short Certificate—Qualified

We have audited the books and accounts of the United States Rubber Company and its subsidiary Companies for the year ended December 31, 1922, excepting those of certain of the foreign subsidiaries, as to which we have accepted reports of other accounting firms and, in some instances, reports of the companies.

The buildings and machinery owned by the Company had a total appraised value at December 31, 1922, after deducting depreciation accrued to that date, which was materially in excess of the value at which they are carried on the books, although depreciation was not fully provided for in connection with the operations of the year 1922; and

WE HEREBY CERTIFY that, subject to the foregoing, the accompanying general balance sheet, in our opinion, correctly sets forth the financial condition of the companies on December 31, 1922, and that the figures relating to the income and surplus accounts referred to in the text of the Chairman's report are correct.

HASKINS & SELLS
Certified Public Accountants

New York
March 8, 1923

15

Procedure concluded that the extended procedures were as applicable to interim statements as they were to year-end statements.

Denial of Opinion. Although SAP No. 1 made clear that the CPA should sometimes withhold an opinion when no opinion could be expressed, the statement tacitly permitted silence in the report concerning the degree of responsibility assumed for the fair presentation of the statements. The statement suggested that the auditor might, if appropriate, give his reasons for omitting the expression of opinion, but an explicit denial of opinion was not required. Many CPAs issued reports which recited their procedures in considerable detail but did not say whether the audit described had satisfied them that the financial statements were fairly presented. The mere absence of remarks concerning the statements was presumed to indicate that the auditor took no responsibility for them.

As a result of this practice, an auditor's report frequently looked exactly the same whether he had prepared financial statements from the accounting records without audit or whether he had made an examination sufficient to express an opinion. In recognition of the need for clarifying reporting responsibilities, the Committee on Auditing Procedure in 1947 issued SAP No. 23—"Recommendation Made to Clarify Accountant's Representations When Opinion Is Not Expressed." For two years the subject was extensively debated by the profession and, in a form revised to reflect issues raised by the debate, the statement was adopted by the membership at the annual meeting of the Institute in 1949 as SAP No. 23 (Revised), "Clarification of Accountant's Report When Opinion Is Omitted." The previously quoted paragraph from "Extensions of Auditing Procedure" was amended and extended as follows:

> The independent certified public accountant should not express the opinion that financial statements present fairly the position of the company and the results of its operations, in conformity with generally accepted accounting principles, when his exceptions are such as to negative the opinion, or when the examination has been less in scope than he considers necessary to express an opinion on the statements taken as a whole. In such circumstances, the independent certified public accountant should state that he is not in a position to express an opinion on the financial statements taken as a whole and should indicate clearly his reasons therefor.

SAP No. 23 also specified the choices available to the auditor in determining what type of report was appropriate and the criteria by which to make the decision:

> Whenever the accountant permits his name to be associated with financial statements, he should determine whether, in the particular circumstances, it is proper for him to (1) express an unqualified opinion, or (2) express a qualified

opinion, or (3) disclaim an opinion on the statements taken as a whole. Thus, when an unqualified opinion cannot be expressed, the accountant must weigh the qualifications or exceptions to determine their significance. If they are not such as to negative the opinion, a properly qualified opinion would be satisfactory; if they are such as to negative an opinion on the statements taken as a whole he should clearly disclaim such an opinion.

The criteria offered for making the reporting decision are notably vague, but the types of reports are, nevertheless, clearly specified. The same position was carried forward without substantive change in two later Institute pronouncements—*Codification of Statements on Auditing Procedure* (1951) and *Generally Accepted Auditing Standards* (1954), in which the position was officially recognized as the fourth standard of reporting. In 1958 the membership, by mail ballot, incorporated the substance of SAP No. 23 in Rule 19 of Rules of Professional Conduct.

Adverse Opinion. Formal identification of a distinct new type of opinion was made in SAP No. 31, "Consistency." Although the subject of SAP No. 31 was, generally, reporting guidelines in applying the consistency standard, a new report category was created, under the caption "change to a principle or practice which lacks general acceptance":

> Where the effect of a change to a principle or practice which is not generally accepted is material, the independent auditor should so state in his report. Such statement requires either a qualification of the independent auditor's opinion as to fair presentation in conformity with generally accepted accounting principles or, if the change is *sufficiently* material, an adverse opinion on the financial statements taken as a whole.

The following note, which appeared in SAP No. 31 beneath an illustration of an adverse opinion, distinguished between an adverse opinion and a disclaimer:

> Since the independent auditor completed his examination in accordance with generally accepted auditing standards, and *has* an opinion (adverse) on the statements, he should not *disclaim* an opinion.

SAP No. 31 was dated October 1961. In the next year—September 1962—SAP No. 32, "Qualifications and Disclaimers," was issued, which contained the following definition of an adverse opinion and the criteria for when one should be issued:

> An adverse opinion is required in any report where the exceptions as to fairness of presentation are so material that in the independent auditor's judgment a qualified opinion is not justified. In such circumstances a disclaimer of opinion *is not* considered appropriate since the independent

auditor has sufficient information to form an opinion that the financial statements are not fairly presented.

Since the Committee on Auditing Procedure had been developing SAP No. 32 for a number of years, it is likely that SAP No. 31 merely anticipated the terminology used in existing drafts of the subsequent statement.

SAP No. 32 was a comprehensive statement on reporting under the fourth standard of reporting. In addition to defining the four distinct types of audit reports (unqualified, qualified, adverse, and disclaimer) the statement discussed unaudited statements, piecemeal opinions, negative assurance, reliance on other auditors, and the distinction between the "except for" and the "subject to" forms of qualification. Within the next year SAP No. 32 was incorporated, without substantive change, as Chapter 10 of SAP No. 33, "Auditing Standards and Procedures."

Identification of adverse opinions in 1961 finally codified a type of report which had been developing over a number of years. *Generally Accepted Auditing Standards* in 1954 gave limited recognition (p. 48) to the possibility of adverse opinions as follows:

> . . . It is possible that cases may occur where the accountant's exceptions as to practices followed by the client are of such significance that he may have reached a definite conclusion that the financial statements do not fairly present the financial position or results of operations. In such cases, he should be satisfied that his report clearly indicates his disagreement with the statements presented.

While this declaration leads directly to an "adverse" opinion, other Institute publications were not as specific, and practice was not uniform. In support of disclosure of an "adverse" view, the Code of Professional Ethics, as amended December 30, 1969, in Rule 2.02 (a) and (b), states:

> In expressing an opinion on representations in financial statements which he has examined, a member or associate may be held guilty of an act discreditable to the profession if . . . he fails to disclose a material fact known to him which is not disclosed in the financial statements but disclosure of which is necessary to make the financial statements not misleading, or . . . he fails to report any material misstatement known to him to appear in the financial statements . . . .

These two required disclosures were contained in the rule when it originally became effective in January 1941.

Despite early recognition of the adverse opinion report category, evidently some CPAs believed that disclaiming an opinion because of the limited character of their examination relieved them of any duty to make affirmative disclosures of known imperfections in the financial statements. In response to an inquiry on this matter, Carman Blough, in the Accounting & Auditing Problems column of *The Journal of Accountancy*, expressed his own views on the question:

> As we indicated in this column some years ago (*Journal of Accountancy*, August, 1951, p. 221), a disclaimer of an opinion by an accountant is, in effect, a statement that he does not have sufficient grounds for forming an opinion as to whether the statements are a fair presentation or not. Merely to state a disclaimer of opinion when he has factual grounds for believing that the financial statements are false or misleading would be hard to justify and we believe the auditor should require adjustment of the accounts or adequate disclosure of the facts. It seems clear to us that if the client is unwilling to make the necessary adjustments or disclosures, the accountant should have nothing to do with the preparation of the financial statements and should positively refuse to permit his name to be associated with them.[3]

One year after the discussion of this situation in Carman Blough's column—February 1959—the committee on professional ethics of the Institute issued Opinion No. 8 acknowledging the fact that Rule 2.02 did not specifically refer to situations in which an opinion was denied, and—in concurrence with Mr. Blough—concluded that:

> In a circumstance where a member believes the financial statements are false or misleading as a whole or in any significant respect, it is the opinion of the committee that he should require adjustments of the accounts or adequate disclosure of the facts, as the case may be, and failing this the independent accountant should refuse to permit his name to be associated with the statements in any way.

Close scrutiny of these precursors of the adverse opinion show that the concept was only partially formed. Although some CPAs did not adhere to the guides, it was clear that a CPA could not discharge his reporting obligation by denying an opinion and conceal the fact that, actually, in his opinion the statements were not fairly presented. However, the sources cited conflicted on whether the CPA should disclose the lack of fair presentation in his report or refuse to be associated with the statements. Also, the main focus was on the situation in which a CPA disclaimed because of the limited nature of his examination and, in addition, was aware of imperfections in the statements.

Both SAP No. 1 and SAP No. 23 indicated that an auditor should withhold any opinion in two situations: (1) when the scope of his examinations was too limited for him to form an opinion, or (2) when he concluded that his exceptions to fair presentation negated an opinion. The implication was that "opinion" meant a favorable

---

[3]*The Journal of Accountancy*, February 1958, p. 68.

(qualified or unqualified) conclusion on the financial statements taken as a whole. In contrast, SAP No. 31 indicated that an *opinion* may be either positive (qualified or unqualified) or negative (adverse).

Trends in Development of Report Types

In viewing the development of report categories over the years in perspective, certain broad trends are discernible.

Origin in Limited Scope. Prior to the pronouncements dealing with adverse opinions, the primary focus of statements on auditing procedure concerned with reporting was the influence of scope limitations on the report. An article prepared by Carman Blough and reviewed by the Committee on Auditing Procedure appeared shortly after the membership approved SAP No. 23.[4] This article attempted to explain the purpose and significance of SAP No. 23, giving primary attention to situations of limited scope. All of the reports in an appendix entitled "Examples of Language Used to Disclaim an Opinion" dealt with an inadequate examination, except for one report on cash basis statements.

Creation of the category of adverse opinion finally gave full recognition to the situation in which the CPA could not give a favorable (qualified or unqualified) opinion on the financial statements taken as a whole even though the scope of his examination was unrestricted. Both SAP No. 1 and SAP No. 23 had acknowledged that an auditor should withhold an opinion "when his exceptions are such as to negative the opinion, or when the examination has been less in scope than he considers necessary." However, there was little elaboration concerning the "exceptions" which might be "such as to negative the opinion." Primary attention focused on the auditor's responsibility to evaluate the completeness of his work. Criteria for evaluating the influence of exceptions to fair presentation on the degree of responsibility assumed were limited to such cryptic comments as "of such importance as to negative an expression of opinion" or "of such extent that they negative . . . . "

When reporting criteria were substantially expanded beyond the problems of limited scope with the issuance of SAP No. 32, the qualitative phrases of "importance," "significance," and "extent" which had been used in earlier pronouncements gave way to the

---

[4]Carman G. Blough, "Significance of Auditing Statement No. 23," *The Journal of Accountancy*, March 1951, pp. 391-401.

all-encompassing modifier "materiality." A qualified opinion is not appropriate if exceptions are "so material" or "sufficiently material."

Recognition of the development of reporting criteria from an origin in problems of scope limitation leads to two observations. First, since the original criteria were based on a restricted scope situation, development of criteria for other situations may have been unduly hampered. The average layman who reads an auditor's report cannot reasonably be expected to evaluate the technical completeness of the auditor's examination. The responsibility for appraising the sufficiency of the examination rests appropriately with the reporting auditor. Early pronouncements on reporting considered it sufficient to require the auditor to withhold an opinion (SAP No. 1) and specifically disclaim an opinion (SAP No. 23) when his examination was inadequate. One revision made in the original text of SAP No. 23 (1947) before it was adopted by the membership in 1949 was the addition of this last paragraph:

> It should be remembered that *Extensions of Auditing Procedure* for 10 years has precluded the expression of any opinion on the financial statements taken as a whole when the accountant's exceptions or qualifications were such as to negative the opinion. That provision is continued under the amendment. The change is concerned solely with improving current reporting practices by providing that, in such cases, the accountant should henceforth clearly indicate that he is not in a position to express an opinion on the financial statements taken as a whole, and give his reasons why.

Thus, the membership was assured that they were adopting a *reporting* requirement. Elaboration in any detail on the audit procedures necessary to support an opinion on the financial statements was considered neither desirable nor feasible. By the time SAP No. 23 was adopted, all Institute pronouncements that had attempted to outline the procedures required in an audit had either been superseded or withdrawn. Consequently, lack of guidance on when a disclaimer of opinion was required because the audit was of insufficient scope was only natural. In addition, the lack of criteria for other exceptions and qualifications was unfortunately continued.

Second, the ascendancy of "materiality" as the primary modifier in reporting criteria in SAP No. 32 probably did not result from an intent to change the criteria from earlier pronouncements. Materiality supplanted all other qualitative terms, including those applied to the adequacy of examination, and the criteria for the scope of the examination certainly did not change.

The conclusion is more tenable that use of "materiality" in reporting criteria simply followed the trend in accounting literature, in general, of substituting "material" for explanations of importance, an inference that has been well-documented elsewhere.[5]

Increasing Standardization. Over the years, writing an audit report has changed from a literary to a coding activity. In the beginning, an auditor, using the descriptive report style, would write a report which was unique for each engagement. An adequate report was one which conveyed the circumstances of the engagement. While qualified certificates were distinguished from unqualified certificates, actually identifying them was an extremely difficult task for the uninitiated. Beginning with the adoption of a standard form for the unqualified opinion, the emphasis changed from the writing of the report to the decision of what type of report was appropriate. The auditor must now choose a report from among four distinct types. Once this decision is made, the words chosen for the report are somewhat constrained by the reporting guidelines of Institute pronouncements. Thus, professional latitude is far greater in the decision-making phase of reporting than in the writing phase.

The transition to standardization is clearly noticeable when SAP No. 23 and SAP No. 32 are compared and contrasted. SAP No. 23 contained the following paragraph:

> It is not contemplated that the disclaimer of an opinion should assume a standardized form. Any expression which clearly states that an opinion has been withheld and gives the reasons why would be suitable for this purpose. However, it is not considered sufficient to state merely that certain auditing procedures were omitted, or that certain departures from generally accepted accounting principles were noted, without explaining their effect upon the accountant's opinion regarding the statements taken as a whole.

Although the same paragraph was included without change in the Codification (1951), subsequent pronouncements—most notably SAP No. 32—do not contain the paragraph, nor any similar statement.

With respect to modifications of the opinion paragraph in the standard short-form report, a provision of SAP No. 32 incorporated as paragraph 11 of Chapter 10 of SAP No. 33 states:

> Any modifying phrases in the standard short-form opinion paragraph (or sentence) should be considered as qualifying the opinion in some manner; however, reference to the report of other independent auditors as the basis, in part, of the opinion whether made in the scope paragraph or the opinion paragraph, is not to be construed as a qualification of the opinion.

---

[5]Warren Reininga, "The Unknown Materiality Concept," *The Journal of Accountancy,* February 1968, pp. 31 and 32.

Thus, any departure from standard wording, with the one exception noted, constitutes a qualified opinion. SAP No. 32 also specified when particular introductory wording ("except for" or "subject to") should be used for qualified opinions.

In contrast to SAP No. 23, which was devoid of examples, SAP No. 32 included examples illustrating the form of all four types of audit reports. The shift to standardization is apparent.

Obviously, *complete* uniformity will never be achieved. All unqualified opinions or all disclaimers of opinion will never be the same, word for word. For example, the financial statements and what they purport to present must be appropriately described. However, when the degree of responsibility assumed by the auditor is changed by his choice of words, differences in language or form not required by the circumstances being reported on are rarely justified.

Consolation Opinions. When the clear requirement for a disclaimer of opinion was established in SAP No. 23, the appropriateness of a "consolation" opinion was simultaneously acknowledged. SAP No. 23 contained the following phrases:

> To the extent the scope of his examination and the findings thereof justify, he may also comment further as to compliance of the statements with generally accepted accounting principles in respects other than those which require the denial of an opinion on the over-all fairness of the financial statements. The purpose of these assertions by the accountant is to indicate clearly the degree of responsibility he is taking.

Although the conclusion is not explicit in SAP No. 23, this phrase was intended to give formal approval to piecemeal opinions. The article interpreting SAP No. 23 referred specifically to piecemeal opinions and related them to the phrase quoted above. The piecemeal opinion seems to have been offered to compensate for the harshness of denial of an opinion, which was required for the first time in 1949.

The underlying rationale seemed to be that a denial of opinion should not necessarily create an impression that no dependence whatever might be placed on the statement or the audit work performed. On balancing the needs of the client with the protection of third parties, the article had this to say with regard to piecemeal opinions:

> The accounting profession in general feels, however, that it has gone as far as it may reasonably be expected to go in the interests of third parties when it requires CPAs who are unable to express an over-all opinion to say so categorically in their reports. It is believed that those who rely upon CPAs' reports will not be misled by any additional comments which fairly clarify the

degree of dependence which may appropriately be placed upon the work actually done.[6]

Discussion prior to this comment had indicated that a "negative assurance" should not be added to a denial of opinion and that the more specific and less confusing piecemeal opinion approach was preferable.

The appropriateness of a "consolation" opinion was closely linked to the service-to-the-client orientation of the profession in this country. Several references to the rights of the client taken from the article interpreting SAP No. 23 suggest the flavor of this orientation:

> It should be borne in mind that CPAs are *engaged to perform services requested by the client.* The client has the right to determine his accounting needs.[7]

> It has been argued that the CPA, not the client, should take responsibility for determining the nature of work which should be done. In view of the fact that it is the client who determines the essential character of the services which he wishes to have performed, this conclusion does not seem supportable. The CPA's responsibility begins after he reaches an agreement with the client on the type of service he is to render. He must then decide what must be done to accomplish the objectives of the engagement.[8]

The literature of the accounting profession is replete with references to the importance of service to management. Many auditing textbook writers emphasize the importance of continual alertness to opportunities to give advice and to make recommendations to management in order to create tangible benefits from the audit other than an audit report. Historically, this service orientation might be traced to the origin of a struggling new auditing profession in this country which may have felt a need to justify engagements on the basis of economic benefits to the client in the absence of any statutory requirements for an audit.

Since clients did not have to have audits, an auditor was not in a position to dictate the extent of work that a client required. The scope of the examination was flexible, but the auditor would, accordingly, restrict his comments to conclusions justified by the scope of work performed. After several decades in which reports were tailored to the circumstances of an engagement, a requirement to specifically deny an opinion on the financial statements taken as a whole when the examination was inadequate may have seemed harsh. To compensate in part, a consolatory piecemeal opinion was approved to soften the impact and avoid casting unwarranted aspersion on the statements.

---

[6] Blough, "Significance of Auditing Statement No. 23," p. 395.
[7] *Ibid.*, p. 391.
[8] *Ibid.*, p. 395.

In addition, a piecemeal opinion could serve a useful purpose for financial statement users by providing positive assurance that the auditor was not aware of any facts which would discredit the financial statements, other than the cause of the disclaimer. In other words, the piecemeal opinion took the place of the discredited negative assurance and assured the report reader that the disclaimer was not used to conceal significant information. It should be remembered that until the matter was clarified in 1961, an auditor had to disclaim an opinion if he could not give a positive opinion (qualified or unqualified) on the statements.

SAP No. 23 had added the following requirement to the admonition in SAP No. 1 concerning the withholding of an opinion:

> In such circumstances, the independent certified public accountant should state that he is not in a position to express an opinion on the financial statements taken as a whole and should indicate clearly his reasons therefor.

In early 1961, a New York practitioner suggested that any legitimate need for consolation opinions in conjunction with disclaimers could be eliminated merely by adding the word "all" to SAP No. 23, as follows: " . . . should indicate clearly *all* his reasons therefor."[9]

He argued that if the auditor were required to state all of his reasons for not being able to express an opinion, a report reader could assume—if the auditor said nothing to the contrary—that the statements were otherwise prepared in conformity with generally accepted accounting principles and that nothing had come to the auditor's attention to cause him to doubt the validity of the amounts in the statements.

This suggested addition to SAP No. 23 was effectively implemented when SAP No. 32 was issued. As incorporated in Chapter 10 of SAP No. 33, the reporting requirements read as follows:

> Whenever the independent auditor issues an adverse opinion, he should disclose *all* the substantive reasons therefor, usually by referring to a middle paragraph of his report describing the circumstances. (Paragraph 13.)

> Whenever the independent auditor disclaims an opinion, he should give *all* substantive reasons for doing so. For example, when he disclaims an opinion because the scope of examination was inadequate, he should also disclose any reservations or exceptions he may have regarding fairness of presentation. (Paragraph 16.)

However, adoption of these requirements was not coupled with a prohibition of piecemeal opinions. In fact, piecemeal opinions were

---

[9] Eugene E. Rosenfeld, "Further Thoughts on the Denial of an Opinion," *The New York Certified Public Accountant,* May 1961, pp. 311-316.

formally recognized in SAP No. 32, with the brief mention in SAP No. 23 expanded to a discussion of several paragraphs. The subject was introduced in SAP No. 33 (Chapter 10, paragraph 22) as follows:

> In some situations requiring a disclaimer of opinion or adverse opinion on the over-all fairness of the financial statements, the auditor may, to the extent that the scope of his examination and the findings thereof justify, express a so-called "piecemeal" opinion as to the compliance of the statements with generally accepted accounting principles in respects other than those which require the disclaimer of opinion or adverse opinion.

With the perspective of the historical development of the consolation opinion in mind, several observations seem worthwhile. First, SAP No. 32 permitted piecemeal opinions in conjunction with adverse opinions almost simultaneously with the creation of the adverse opinion. Before SAP No. 32, piecemeal opinions were given only in conjunction with disclaimers of opinion since that was the only type of report which an auditor could issue when he could not express a positive opinion. When the adverse opinion category was created, piecemeal opinions were immediately permitted in conjunction with adverse ones, without any experience in using the new report category. On reflection, one can question whether an auditor should give positive approval to parts of statements when he has concluded that the financial statements taken as a whole are not fairly presented and the client has refused to modify the statements. Since the social need furnished by the auditor is that of facilitating the flow of reliable financial information to statement users, when a client acts to thwart the dissemination of reliable information, is a consolation opinion warranted?

Second, more than two decades have passed since the requirement for a specific denial of opinion was adopted by the membership. The justification for softening the impact of a denial on a client accustomed to a report of comments justified by the scope of work may no longer exist.

Finally, the policy decision made over two decades ago that the profession had gone as far as it could in protecting third parties by requiring a specific denial probably has little relevance in today's financial environment. The requirement to disclose all substantive reasons for not giving a positive opinion now assures a report reader that an adverse opinion or disclaimer is not being used to conceal other relevant information. In addition, the protection of third-party interests has assumed far more importance than it had over twenty years ago.

Recognition of Unusual Uncertainties. Although auditors in practice were faced with the problem of evaluating unusual uncertainties, Institute pronouncements on reporting gave scant attention to the subject before the issuance of SAP No. 32 in late 1962. SAPs No. 1 and 23 gave no guidance on the possible types of exceptions, except for the following paragraph from SAP No. 1:

> Any exception should be expressed clearly and unequivocally as to whether it affects the scope of the work, any particular item of the financial statements, the soundness of the company's procedures (as regards either the books or the financial statements), or the consistency of accounting practices where lack of consistency calls for exception.

As early as 1915, however, George O. May in his article on qualifications in certificates had—as the following passage indicates—clearly recognized the problem, although his solution leaves a bit to be desired:

> There are, of course, cases where the value of certain assets or the amount of certain liabilities is so uncertain that neither auditors nor directors can form definite opinions. If in such cases the best judgment of the auditor differs from that of the directors, or if the auditor is not prepared either to endorse the directors' opinions or express one of his own, a statement of the facts and of the directors' views thereon may, it would seem, properly be embodied in the audit certificate. An alternative course which has often proved convenient and satisfactory to all concerned is for the auditor to agree with directors on a statement to be made by the latter in their report to stockholders regarding the special point involved and for the auditor then to certify that the accounts, "read in conjunction with the explanation regarding _____ contained in the directors' report, set forth, etc."[10]

In contrast, the only Institute pronouncement which dealt with the influence of uncertainties was SAP No. 15, "Disclosure of the Effect of Wartime Uncertainties on Financial Statements." This statement recognized that serious uncertainties were created by the possible effect of renegotiation of war contracts, and that as a result of war damage to property "insurance claims may have been filed, or may subsequently be filed, the ultimate outcome of which is uncertain." The advice given on disclosure of uncertainties in the auditor's report was as follows:

> With respect to material uncertainties, three types of situations, among others, may be contemplated:
> (1) The case in which the auditor believes that the financial statements, so far as possible, present fairly the position and the results of operations, but feels that the uncertainties are such that special attention should be drawn to them in his report, as well as in the statements themselves, but without taking an exception.

---

[10]May, "Qualifications in Certificates," pp. 253-254.

(2) The case in which one or more uncertainties are such as to require an exception.

(3) The case in which the cumulative effect of the uncertainties is so great that no opinion is possible, although the auditor may be able to make a statement as to the extent to which he approves the statements and the reasons for omitting the usual opinion on the statements as a whole.

In other words, an uncertainty could result in an unqualified opinion, a qualified opinion, or a withheld opinion, but no criteria for these alternatives were offered.

In the absence of guidance from Institute pronouncements, auditing firms developed reporting manuals to cover the various types of exceptions and their treatment in audit reports. A book based on an audit firm manual and published in 1955 listed the following categories for exceptions: (1) limitations on the scope of the examination, (2) failure to follow generally accepted accounting principles, (3) lack of consistency in the accounting principles followed, and (4) the existence of contingencies whose effect neither the company nor the auditor can determine at the date of the report.[11] Examples given of qualifications based on contingencies included realization of receivables, outcome of a lawsuit, income taxes, value of pledged property, and determination of rates for a regulated company.

The qualified opinions illustrating these examples used the introductory phrases "except for" and "subject to" interchangeably. In fact, two Institute publications prepared to explain audit reports to nonaccountants, "40 Questions and Answers About Audit Reports" (1956) and "Audits by Certified Public Accountants" (1950), both illustrate opinions qualified for uncertainties using an "except for" introduction.

A review of reports issued in the early 1950s indicates that "subject to" and "except for" were used interchangeably for *all* types of exceptions. Although "except for" was considered a more forceful exception, the phrase could be applied to any exception. Thus degrees of qualification existed unofficially within the category of qualified opinions.

The difficulty of assessing the significance of qualifying phrases in the opinion paragraph was undoubtedly an important factor in the SEC's issuance of Accounting Series Release No. 90. The pertinent portion of ASR No. 90 reads as follows:

A "subject to" or "except for" opinion paragraph in which these phrases refer to the scope of the audit, indicating that the accountant has not been able to satisfy himself on some significant element in the financial statements,

---

[11] Jennie M. Palen, *Report Writing For Accountants*, Prentice-Hall, Inc., Englewood Cliffs, N.J., 1955, p. 360.

is not acceptable in certificates filed with the Commission in connection with the public offering of securities. The "subject to" qualification is appropriate when the reference is to a middle paragraph or to footnotes explaining the status of matters which cannot be resolved at statement date.

In analyzing ASR No. 90, Carman Blough agreed with the SEC's limitations on the use of "subject to" qualifications:

It has been our opinion for many years, dating back to pre-SEC days, that the words "subject to" in an opinion paragraph were so ambiguous that they conveyed no clear-cut meaning to the reader. There is no way of telling whether they are intended to be a qualification of the opinion, or whether they are intended merely to direct the attention of the reader to some significant fact which has been more fully disclosed elsewhere. The circumstances in which Release No. 90 indicates that the SEC will tolerate the use of this expression in the opinion paragraph seem to us to be about the only ones in which we could justify its use. The same lack of clarity of intent is present when the phrase "with the foregoing explanation" is used in connection with the opinion. Is it intended that this expression shall merely indicate that the explanation itself is so important to a full understanding of the statement that special attention has to be drawn to it, or does it mean that the auditor is taking an exception to the fairness of the presentation of the financial statements themselves?[12]

When the Committee on Auditing Procedure issued reporting guidelines for the treatment of uncertainties in SAP No. 32, they adopted a similar position. As incorporated in Chapter 10 of SAP No. 33, the requirements read:

The use of phrases that include either "except" or "exception" in qualified opinions on financial statements is recommended. However, in certain cases where the outcome of a matter is uncertain the phrase "subject to" may be appropriate . . . . Phrases such as "with the foregoing explanation" are generally not clear or forceful enough for a qualification and should not be used to qualify an opinion. (Paragraph 10.)

Uncertainties are present when limitations on the scope of the examination are imposed, but such uncertainties are not of the nature and type which permit the use of "subject to" in qualifying the opinion . . . . (Paragraph 30.)

The committee, however, was not simply endorsing the SEC's position. According to Mr. Blough's analysis of ASR No. 90, the committee had been preparing a statement on reporting for a number of years:

It is our understanding that, although the committee had not taken definitive action on the proposed statement, a copy of a preliminary draft was submitted informally to the accounting staff of the SEC for comment some

---

[12]"SEC Release on Opinions and Opening Inventories," *The Journal of Accountancy*, May 1962, p. 72.

time before the issuance of [A]ccounting Series Release No. 90 and that the staff and the committee were in complete agreement on this particular phase of the statement.[13]

The interchange between the committee and the SEC on the appropriate use of the "subject to" qualification has continued over the years. The "subject to" qualification is discussed in two more releases, No. 115 and No. 118, which are considered at a later point.

Thus, the role of unusual uncertainties in reporting guidelines changed from a position of relative obscurity to one of careful prescription. Two observations on this transition are pertinent. First, the connection between the qualifying phrase "subject to" and an unusual uncertainty having an impact on the statements is largely arbitrary. Until 1962, the only recognized distinction between a "subject to" and an "except for" qualification was that the latter was more forceful. Conceivably, an uncertainty could be important enough to the proper interpretation of financial statements to require the most forceful form of qualification possible. The distinction introduced by SAP No. 32 is largely artificial.

Second, the position of the SEC on the "subject to" form of qualification has probably caused that qualifying phrase to have undue significance. According to ASR No. 90, the only form of qualification "acceptable in certificates filed with the Commission in connection with the public offering of securities" is one which makes reference to "the status of matters which cannot be resolved at statement date." SAP No. 32 designated these qualifications based on uncertainties as the only qualifications in which a "subject to" introduction was appropriate. Consequently, the phrase "subject to" has assumed the status of a watchword for a qualification acceptable to the SEC. In contrast to other forms of qualification, a qualifying phrase with a "subject to" introduction does not result in an "unacceptable certificate." Conceivably, more importance attaches to the words used to introduce the qualification than to its substance.

Summary

The evolution of report categories leading to the present guidelines for the implementation of the fourth reporting standard found in Chapter 10 of SAP No. 33 had distinct stages. In chronological order these stages were:

1. 1934: Recommendation of a short-form report as a "standard" from which departures would have a recognizable significance.

---

[13] *Ibid.*

2. 1939: A requirement in SAP No. 1 that an auditor should *withhold* an opinion when his exceptions or the inadequate scope of his examination negate an overall opinion.

3. 1949: A requirement in SAP No. 23 that an auditor should categorically *disclaim* an opinion when he could not express one.

4. 1961: Creation of a new category of report—adverse opinion—in SAP No. 31.

5. 1962: The present position, originally in SAP No. 32, now incorporated in SAP No. 33.

Listing the developments makes another trend apparent—the increasing explicitness of reporting guidelines. Specifying that an opinion should not be expressed in certain circumstances was not enough. The need to disclaim also had to be specified. Requiring the auditor to disclose the reasons for a disclaimer was insufficient. An adverse category of reports had to be articulated to avoid concealment of important information. Knowledge of this history creates an expectation that new guidelines will be more explicit than previous pronouncements.

Other expectations created by an analysis of the trends in the evolution of reporting are as follows:

1. While limited guidelines are justified for evaluating the adequacy of the scope of an examination, more explicit guidelines are necessary for situations involving uncertainties or departures from generally accepted accounting principles.

2. Qualitative phrases such as "so material" do not convey the necessary connotation of *importance,* and additional criteria for making the report-type decision should be developed.

3. Since relatively minor changes in the language used in an audit report change the responsibility assumed by the auditor, the standardization of report form and wording should increase.

4. While the justification for permitting use of the piecemeal opinion may have been sufficient in 1949, that justification does not continue today, and piecemeal opinions should probably be restricted further.

5. Since present distinctions between appropriate use of "subject to" and "except for" are largely artificial, emphasis needs to be placed on the substance of a qualification rather than the phrase used to introduce it.

3

Legal Liability and the Language of Reports

The purpose of the audit report is to communicate to the reader the CPA's professional opinion on the financial statements identified in the report, and either clients or third parties may seek to impose liability on the CPA for his report representations. Proper identification of the type of report rendered is essential since the literature of the profession explains in detail the meaning of the opinion expressed, if any, by each type of report. Thus, the critical role of the choice of report language used by the auditor cannot be overemphasized.

If the type of report rendered is properly identified, the CPA is protected against the appearance of assuming responsibility he does not intend to assume. For example, a court in New York has held that if a CPA prepares financial statements for a client on the CPA's letterhead and attaches no audit report or disclaimer limiting the extent to which the figures in the statements have been audited, the statements will be treated as audited financial statements. The court referred to the fourth standard of reporting and concluded that:

> ... Defendants' failure to place any qualification notice on the subject balance sheet, therefore, clearly constituted a violation of the emphasized portion of the cited rule which, without any doubt, fixes the existing and accepted standards of the profession.
>
> The balance sheet on the defendants' professional letterhead was unqualified and in effect, an audited financial statement upon which plaintiff had the right to rely in order to determine and evaluate its financial condition as of April 30, 1957. It is clear that in order to relieve themselves of liability for errors contained in this April 30, 1957 balance sheet, defendants could have and should have indicated on its face all items that were not independently verified.[1]

---

[1] *Stanley L. Bloch, Inc.* v. *Klein*, 258 N.Y.S. 2d 501 (1965), pp. 506-507.

In a legal action against an auditor, his audit report assumes special importance. The plaintiff's action may be for the tort of misrepresentation (either fraudulent or negligent), or, in an action by the client, for breach of contract. Any restrictions or limitations on the opinion must be clearly stated in the audit report, and the auditor will have the burden of explaining away any ambiguities.

Although many legal cases involving the liability of independent public accountants exist, few cases shed light on the question of the responsibility assumed when the audit report expresses limitations on the scope of the examination or on the opinion as they relate to one or more material items affecting the financial statements taken as a whole. An auditor will at times have to limit his responsibility in this respect. However, assessment of the effect of the type of report issued on liability is difficult without reference to actual cases in which the meaning of a qualification or disclaimer was at issue.

Qualified Opinions and Liability

Three cases—two involving the same audit report—have dealt with the liability of a public accountant when a qualified opinion is expressed.

The C.I.T. Case.[2] The C.I.T. Financial Corporation alleged that the bankruptcy of Manufacturers Trading Corporation, a finance company to whom they had loaned money, had resulted in loss and that the auditor's report had misrepresented MTC's financial position. They complained that the audit was deficient since it did not disclose that the borrower's accounts receivable were overvalued, and that a large provision for uncollectible accounts should have been made because of the stagnancy of collateral.

The auditors contended that they had not assumed any competence to appraise the collateral and called attention to a qualifying phrase in the audit report which stated:

> While it was not within our province to pass upon or assume responsibility for the legal or equitable title to the commercial receivables purchased by the companies or the valuation of any security thereto accepted and held by them, it was apparent from their books and records and by opinion of counsel that their contractual and assignment forms are adequate for their legal protection in connection with the collection and liquidation of commercial receivables purchased.

The audit report in question was dated June 30, 1945, and a similar or identical statement was included in other reports, the last of which was

---

[2] *C.I.T. Financial Corporation* v. *Glover, et al.*, 224 F. 2d 44 (2d Cir. 1955).

for the period ended June 30, 1948. The audit report was of a type, common at the time, which might be called "descriptive"—a cross between a short-form and a long-form report. The plaintiff received the same detailed report that was given to the client. Following the scope paragraph was a listing of the accounting and operating practices of MTC and the related matters of audit scope. Included in the list was the limiting phrase quoted above. Although this phrase was referred to as a "disclaimer" in the case, it should not be confused with a disclaimer of opinion on the financial statements taken as a whole.

The plaintiff argued that the auditor's qualification merely denied responsibility for the valuation of collateral, but the jury, finding for the defendant-accountants, applied it equally to the valuation of collateral and accounts receivable. On appeal the court held that the meaning of the report was properly left to the jury to decide, and the Court of Appeals affirmed the judgment of the lower court.

The following excerpt from Judge Ryan's charge to the jury in the initial trial indicates the opposing views of the meaning of the report language:

> Defendants contend that by this disclaimer or qualification anyone who read their reports would take notice that the defendants assumed no responsibility for the valuation of the collateral held by Manufacturers Trading Corporation. This much plaintiff apparently concedes, but plaintiff contends that this disclaimer did not permit the defendants to close their eyes to facts and to give up the alertness which an accountant should apply during his audit.
>
> Plaintiff contends that if the defendants had reasonable ground to suspect that the collateral was not worth the amounts which the management thought it was worth, the disclaimer did not cover the situation. There was testimony of expert accounting witnesses bearing on the issue. The question of the accounting principles involved is a question of fact which you, as jurors, are to decide and the true meaning and application of the disclaimer or qualification, in light of that testimony and the other facts of the case, is for you to decide.

The plaintiff also challenged the appropriateness of the *type* of report issued. In the following passage from the charge to the jury, plaintiff in effect asserts that the report should have contained a disclaimer of opinion on the financial statements taken as a whole rather than a qualified opinion:

> Plaintiff contends that on the fair reading of the language of the disclaimer in light of standard accounting practices it does not extend to the valuation of the receivables. Plaintiff further urges that the defendants expressed an opinion on the valuation of the receivables when they expressed their opinion that the balance sheet presented the financial condition of Manufacturers Trading Corporation and its subsidiary with a reserve for

doubtful accounts set forth against the receivables. Defendants answer that the remarks about the reserve for doubtful accounts in the body of its report were not their own representations, but were those of the management, and that this was made clear by the comments in the reports.

Plaintiff contends, however, that it is a principle of auditing that if an accountant withholds an expression of opinion on so large a portion of the total assets of the enterprise as to amount to a withholding of the expression of an opinion on the financial statements as a whole, the accountant has no right, as a matter of auditing principle, to express any opinion on the financial statements, and he must refrain from signing a report. Since the receivables amounted to over 80 per cent of the total assets of Manufacturers Trading Corporation, plaintiff contends that this asserted auditing principle is applicable here. Therefore, plaintiff contends, both as a matter of the reading of the report by itself, and on the basis of the report in the light of the foregoing asserted auditing principle that the defendants did express an opinion on the valuation of the receivables. On these points, both parties offered expert accounting testimony, and the defendants vigorously contend that the qualified opinion was entirely proper in view of the very nature of Manufacturers' business, of the special skill and experience of Alfred H. Sachs, its president, in the realization upon collateral which the company had in the past been obliged to possess and liquidate when large loans secured by collateral were in default.

As with the other contentions of the plaintiff, these issues were left for the jury to decide.

Thus, in the *C.I.T.* case where the meaning of the qualification in the audit report was left to their decision, the jury found for the CPA. In another case involving the same report, the judge ruled on the meaning of the qualification, and the jury found for the plaintiff.

The First Bank Case. In *First Bank and Trust Company of South Bend* v. *Small et. al.,*[3] another of MTC's creditors contended—and the jury found—that the auditors had knowingly and fraudulently issued reports which did not show MTC's true financial position since they failed to disclose that approximately 30 per cent of the total assets consisted of loans made to MTC's president's brother and to other companies which he controlled.

In contrast to the *C.I.T.* case in which the meaning of the qualification was left to the jury, in *First Bank* Judge Greenberg refused to admit testimony concerning the meaning of the report, ruling that its meaning was a matter of law and that it had no bearing on the issue of defendants' liability. Speaking of the same report as did Judge Ryan in

---

[3] 6 A.D. 2d 679 (1st Dep't. 1958). This case is unreported, but is discussed in R.W.V. Dickerson, *Accountants and the Law of Negligence*, The Canadian Institute of Chartered Accountants, Toronto, 1966, pp. 23-28.

the *C.I.T.* case, Judge Greenberg charged the jury as follows:

I shall charge you as a matter of law with the meaning of this disclaimer clause and you must accept the Court's ruling in respect to this disclaimer clause in your deliberations in the jury room. The clause means that the defendant accountants do not assume to act and have not acted as lawyers in respect to the legal validity of the documents evidencing or supporting the commercial receivables or as appraisers with respect to the valuation of collateral, and that it was not their function or responsibility to do so; that is to say, they were not lawyers, they were not appraisers. They were not required, for example, nor were they responsible for determining whether or not the documents relating to the assignment of the collateral to MTC as security were valid documents which gave the company a legally enforceable security title to the collateral. Nor was it their function to appraise the items of collateral and set their own valuation on it. This is what the disclaimer clause means, and nothing more.

Plaintiff here makes no claim that it was the defendants' responsibility either to pass upon legal matters nor to appraise the collateral or that they are liable to plaintiff in damage because they failed to do so. It is plaintiff's claim that the defendants are liable because they knew but failed to disclose in their report certain facts having a material bearing on the company's financial condition, without which disclosure they could not, and knowingly or recklessly did not, fairly present MTC's financial condition.

I charge you, therefore, that as to this claim of the plaintiff, the disclaimer clause has no bearing whatsoever on the issue of the defendants' liability, if you conclude that the claim of the plaintiff is a proper one and you accept it on the basis of the facts as announced to you and as shall be announced to you and the statement of law which I shall give you.

I charge you further that the disclaimer clause did not in any way relieve the defendants of their responsibility to investigate further or to make disclosure of any material matter discovered by them, where such investigation or disclosure were reasonably required. If they saw anything questionable or suspicious with respect to any situation having a material bearing on Manufacturers Trading financial condition, the defendants were required, if they made no disclosure to get to the bottom of it and satisfy themselves that, according to proper auditing and reporting principles, no such disclosure was required.

As bearing on the question whether the defendants had knowledge that the collateral was not worth the amounts which the management represented, the plaintiff offered evidence principally with respect to several accounts, all of which were so-called liquor accounts.

Plaintiff offered evidence, as I recall it, which, it contended, tended to show that certain liquors of Imported Liquors Company and Distilled Liquors Company were slow moving and had fallen in market value.

The defendants deny that these conclusions are to be drawn from the evidence or that they had knowledge of them or their effect upon the value of the collateral, and allege that they plainly stated that they were accepting management's valuation of these goods, and that they, as accountants, were not and did not appraise them. This, of course, is a question of fact which you, as jurors, are called upon to decide.

The difference in the legal effect of the language in the auditor's report may be explained by important differences in the issues raised. In contrast to the *C.I.T.* case, the plaintiff in the *First Bank* case did not argue that the auditors had assumed responsibility for the value of the receivables. Consequently, the meaning of the qualification was not at issue. Rather than arguing that MTC's assets were overstated, they contended that the 1947 and 1948 reports did not fairly present MTC's financial position because the auditors knowingly failed to disclose the concentration of loans to the president's brother, which had a material impact on financial position. While these facts were extremely important to a prospective creditor, they were probably of less concern to C.I.T., who relied on the post-1945 reports primarily to determine if it had a right to accelerate the maturity of its loan because of a drop in MTC's net worth below a stipulated amount.

The Stephens Industries Case. In an action by a buyer of a car rental business against public accountants for alleged misrepresentation of the status of accounts receivable in audited financial statements, a qualified opinion was involved.[4] The sellers of the car rental business employed the auditing firm to make a full scope audit, but in the course of the examination it became apparent that the accounts-receivable records had not been properly maintained and that a discrepancy existed between the detail of the accounts-receivable records and the general ledger. After attempting, unsuccessfully, to reconcile the two records, the auditors informed the client of the additional time and costs required to complete the examination of the accounts receivable.

The auditors were then shown the purchase contract which specifically stated that the accounts receivable were not to be adjusted to reflect uncollectibility. In view of the explicit language of the purchase contract and at the instruction of the client, requests for confirmation of accounts receivable were not sent; the general ledger was adjusted to the balance of the detail records; and no examination of collectibility was made. An appropriately qualified opinion was expressed with the scope paragraph modified as follows:

> Our examination was made in accordance with generally accepted auditing standards, and accordingly included such tests of the accounting records and such other auditing procedures as we considered necessary in the circumstances, excepting that in accordance with your instructions we did not request any of the customers to confirm their balances nor did we review the collectibility of any trade accounts receivable.

---

[4] *Stephens Industries, Inc.* v. *Haskins and Sells,* 438 F. 2d 357 (10th Cir. 1971).

In addition, the balance sheet contained the following note:

> The balance shown on the balance sheet is the total of the detail accounts receivable records of the companies and has not been adjusted to reflect uncollectible accounts, the amount of which was not determined at December 31, 1964.

The trial court ruled for the auditors, and the plaintiff-buyers appealed the case. The Court of Appeals ruled on several matters in affirming the decision of the trial court. With respect to the significance of the qualified opinion, the court stated:

> ...the care and competence of appellees is reflected in the notes attached to the balance sheet and in the separate accountants' opinion. In both places the accountants explicitly recited that the accounts receivable had not been adjusted to reflect collectibility.
>
> From this evidence we are satisfied that appellees exercised the care and competence required of their profession. They followed the scope of audit as outlined by their clients, and carefully limited their work product results to coincide exactly with the undertaking.

It should be noted, however, that the auditors' qualification was only a part—albeit an extremely important one—of their successful defense. The language of the purchase contract, as well as the proper writeoff of accounts known to be uncollectible, were also important elements of the defense.

Also of interest is the fact that the court upheld the privity of contract doctrine. This aspect of the case is tempered by the fact that the case was decided under Colorado law. Federal jurisdiction was conferred by reason of diversity of citizenship, and the federal court was required to define and apply applicable state law.

The Court of Appeals thus upheld the trial court's application of the *Ultramares* doctrine, requiring proof of fraud by a plaintiff not in privity with the accountant defendants. However, the Court also indicated that the evidence established that the auditors had exercised due care.

Summary. All three cases have implications for interpreting the legal effect of a qualified opinion. Since the meaning of a qualification may be left to the decision of a jury, the wording of the qualification should be unequivocal. In a qualified opinion, the auditor attempts to limit his responsibility for some specified aspect of the financial statements. The qualification should state precisely the nature and effect of the exception on the financial statements. In the *First Bank* case, the judge ruled that a qualification on one aspect of receivables did not remove all responsibility for the presentation of receivables. In view of this decision, there seems to be a substantive question of whether a disclaimer of opinion would have been appropriate, and, as such, would have afforded greater legal protection.

Disclaimers of Opinion and Liability

When the disclaimer results from extensive limitations on the scope of the work and the statements are unaudited, no difficulty should be encountered, provided the disclaimer is clear and un-equivocal.[5] However, when the limitation relates only to one or a few material accounts, there may be a problem in determining what legal liability is avoided by denying an opinion on the financial statements taken as a whole. What if misstatements exist in accounts other than, and unrelated to, the accounts on which the disclaimer is based?

The Grain Storage Investigation. Although no known legal case deals precisely with the meaning of this sort of disclaimer of opinion, a proceeding of a subcommittee of the Committee on Government Operations of the House of Representatives may have some bearing on the issue. The passages of testimony (of Winn P. Jackson) reproduced below could easily be read as the cross-examination of a CPA on trial. The testimony of the CPA was part of the investigation of the financial entanglements of Billie Sol Estes—a Pecos, Texas, businessman, who through a complex of irregular operations had defrauded several of the largest finance companies in the country. Estes was involved in a series of grain warehousing agreements with the Department of Agriculture; the Department requested Estes to furnish an audited financial statement and, subsequently, relied upon the audit report introduced at the beginning of the following excerpt from the House proceedings on May 28, 1962:

> MR. FOUNTAIN. So you prepared this statement on your stationery, with the firm name Jackson & Rogers, certified public accountants?
>
> MR. JACKSON. Right.
>
> MR. FOUNTAIN. Lubbock, Tex. Will you read that statement to us and state whether or not the attached sheets were also prepared by him and whether or not that is an exact copy of the information which he furnished to you to be supplied him over your signature?

---

[5]The *1136 Tenants'* case involved unaudited statements included in the CPA's transmittal letter which contained a disclaimer of opinion, but not the disclaimer recommended by the Committee on Auditing Procedure. *1136 Tenants' Corp.* v. *Max Rothenberg & Company,* 84 A.D. 2d 804, 319 N.Y.S. 2d 1007 (1971).

MR. JACKSON (reading):

Mr. Billie Sol Estes,
Pecos, Tex.

DEAR SIR: We have examined the balance sheet presented in condensed form of Billie Sol Estes as of December 31, 1960. Our examination was made in accordance with generally accepted auditing standards and accordingly included such tests of the accounting records and such other auditing procedures as we considered necessary in these circumstances; except that our examination did not include the generally accepted auditing procedure of observing and testing the methods used in determining inventory quantities, prices, and amounts.

By reason of the limitation of the scope of our examination as to inventories, no opinion may be expressed as to the fairness of the presentation in the accompanying balance sheet of the financial position of Billie Sol Estes as of December 31, 1960.

Respectfully,

JACKSON & ROGERS,
By WINN P. JACKSON,
Certified Public Accountant.

(Dated) February 14, 1961.

* * *

MR. FOUNTAIN. Did you make any examinations of books or records of any kind or nature or description before preparing that statement?

MR. JACKSON. No, sir; I did not.

MR. FOUNTAIN. You simply submitted the statement which he had prepared in the form in which he had prepared it and mailed it to him?

MR. JACKSON. Right. At the time I certainly didn't have any reason to doubt his net worth.

MR. FOUNTAIN. Let me ask you this question. As a certified public accountant, just what does that statement mean?

MR. JACKSON. As a certified public accountant, that means that—nothing, in effect, because of the fact it says—

No opinion may be expressed as to the fairness of presentation in the accompanying balance sheet of the financial position of Billie Sol Estes.

Now, that is what accountants or CPAs refer to as a disclaimer, because of the fact they have not been able to examine statements or records sufficiently to warrant giving an opinion, or even a qualified opinion.

MR. SMITH. But the disclaimer only went to inventories, didn't it?

MR. JACKSON. No. The description of the work done on the described inventory. But the disclaimer says no opinion may be expressed, and that applies to all the assets and liabilities. I didn't feel like I could give any other kind of report or opinion other than a disclaimer.

MR. FOUNTAIN. Of course you said—

We have examined the balance sheet presented in condensed form of Billie Sol Estes as of December 31, 1960.

Did you examine the balance sheet?

MR. JACKSON. Right.

MR. FOUNTAIN. And the balance sheet was identical with this?

MR. JACKSON. Right; except let me point out one item. For instance, I think land and depreciable assets he had listed like fixed assets, and I just called it land and depreciable assets. That is the caption I liked better, but I didn't change anything else as far as the figures.

MR. FOUNTAIN. But he presented you no balance sheet which contained any more information than is contained on these sheets?

MR. JACKSON. That's right.

MR. FOUNTAIN. Now, you state—

Our examination was made in accordance with generally accepted auditing standards.

You say you made no examination?

MR. JACKSON. Except—there's a semicolon there.

MR. FOUNTAIN (reading):

And accordingly included such tests of the accounting records and such other auditing procedures as we considered necessary in the circumstances.

What would a certified public accountant have in mind when he says—

included such tests of the accounting records and such other auditing procedures as we considered necessary in the circumstances.

MR. JACKSON. First of all, every audit that you make is different, see; and an auditor has to decide when he gets into the audit as to how much or what extent he carries his procedures, because if you get into making an audit of a company and they have good internal control, checks and balances and such, you wouldn't carry your audit procedures to such an extent as opposed to another audit that you did for a company and they didn't have good internal control or good checks and balances.

Then also, there are many times when you get into doing an audit perhaps you run into something that maybe you feel you need to extend certain auditing procedures. So that's the reason you say, "In the circumstances." You felt it to be necessary in the circumstances.

MR. FOUNTAIN. And then you say—

except that our examination did not include the generally accepted auditing procedures in determining inventory quantities, prices, and amounts.

Now, what did you mean by that?

MR. JACKSON. Well, of course, the request came to us after the first of the year; and the balance sheet, being presented as of December 31, 1960, we could not go back and observe or test the inventories as of that date because that date had already passed and it would just be an impossibility.

So we had no means at all or no reason to give any kind of an idea otherwise.

MR. FOUNTAIN. Now you say in your next paragraph that—

no opinion may be expressed as to the fairness of the presentation of the accompanying balance sheet of the financial position of Billie Sol Estes as of December 31, 1960.

Now, I am putting the first part of it at the end for emphasis—"by reason of the limitation of the scope of our examination as to inventories." Just what would normally be meant by that?

MR. JACKSON. Exactly that no opinion was being rendered at all on the financial position of Mr. Billie Sol Estes as of December 31, 1960.

MR. FOUNTAIN. Why was that stated, "by reason of the scope of our examination as to inventory." What does that mean?

MR. JACKSON. Our profession requires that before we can render an opinion on a financial statement that we must do two positive things, and that is (1) that we must observe and test the inventories—and what I mean by that is that when the company is taking their inventory at the end of their accounting year we must be there to observe and satisfy ourselves that it is all counted and listed. And when we test them, the prices, we go back to their purchase invoice and data to get the cost to compare with their prices that they use to make the extensions of the amounts.

MR. SMITH. Doesn't that indicate that you are satisfied that he has the assets that he says, except that you don't know whether or not he has his inventory?

MR. JACKSON. No. Any time an accountant—at least, the layman might misunderstand, just like a lot of us don't understand a lot of things about law, you know. But any CPA, when you say no opinion may be expressed, regardless of what your reasons or what you did or didn't do, when you get down and say "No opinion may be expressed," it means exactly that and nothing else.

MR. SMITH. This is accountancy jargon, then that means something doesn't necessarily look like it means?

MR. JACKSON. No; I wouldn't say that. It should be obvious to anyone that when you say no opinion may be expressed, that that is exactly the meaning.

MR. FOUNTAIN. You are saying by reason of one item, but actually you are expressing no opinion as to the fairness of presentation in the accompanying balance sheet of the financial position of Billie Sol Estes as of December 31, 1960.

MR. JACKSON. Right.

MR. FOUNTAIN. Mr. Hanna is a [CPA] who is associated with the subcommittee in its investigation. I will yield to you, Mr. Hanna.

MR. HANNA. ... In your "scope" paragraph you said that you made the tests to the extent that you deemed necessary and, as a result of those tests, you are qualifying the scope because inventory could not be tested. Therefore, in your "opinion" paragraph you are stating that, because of the limitation of your scope and inventory, you may not express an opinion.

Now, what about materiality? We have inventory that is less than $1 million. We have total assets that are $20 million. Do you consider inventory to be a material item in that respect?

MR. JACKSON. Well, I did not—I do not know whether I would or not. Of course, as I look at it, when you get into checking inventories a lot of times you pick up other errors, many errors in other accounts. And inventory usually is a big item for an accountant to consider and look at, regardless of how small or how large a company is.

And certainly—I probably, from inexperience—maybe I could have written a report that would have been a little plainer, you know, to the average person to read. But at the same time, I was endeavoring, to the best of my ability, to get the fact over that I could not express an opinion in his financial statement.

MR. HANNA. There were other assets that were much more material than inventory. Now, if your tests were as necessary under the circumstances, then you, by reason of deduction, must have necessarily assured yourself that the other assets were reasonably fair as a result of your tests.

MR. JACKSON. Well, not necessarily. In my own mind thinking, because, not having been able to examine inventories to me was a big item at that time. And I felt like, for that reason, that I could not express an opinion on it.

MR. HANNA. But we had land stated in there, I believe, somewhat in the area of $2 million. Now, the effect that your scope has is to say that the tests that you made, under the circumstances, you had no question whatsoever about. Had you had a question, you were required, under the rules of your profession, to make full disclosure. And you only qualified for inventory—a rather insignificant item.

MR. JACKSON. Well, I might—it might—ended up being worded that way, but it was not meant that way, in my own mind at the time.

* * *

MR. HANNA. What prompted you to select inventory? Were you aware of what the bulk of Mr. Estes' income was? Did inventory play a principal part in producing income for Mr. Estes?

MR. JACKSON. Well, I did not really know at the time what most of his income was from.

MR. HANNA. So inventory, then, you could not say whether or not it was material?

MR. JACKSON. Well, I felt like that anytime according to the rules and regulations of the profession that I have read that we could never give any other kind of a report on anybody, other than a disclaimer like that, unless we had observed and tested the inventories, see. So I was merely complying with that regulation as I understood it.

* * *

MR. LANGEN. Just let me ask this of you as an accountant. Suppose you were at the other end of the line and received a report like this, worded the way that one is. What would that mean to you when you got that? Would this be something that you would rely on as an accounting of a man's interests and his net worth?

MR. JACKSON. No, sir. As an accountant, I would file it in the wastebasket as far as depending on it for anything. Because any time that you cannot get a CPA to express an opinion, you cannot depend on the audit work or what was done to establish the figures that are—is the way I understand it.

MR. SMITH. Don't CPAs generally limit the scope of their opinion?

MR. JACKSON. Oh, I do not know what the general—I would not say whether that would be general or not.

MR. FOUNTAIN. You could just say, based on the examination of the information supplied by the man for whom you were making the audit?

MR. JACKSON. That is right. There are many unqualified opinions given, in which they say, you know, everything is right, as far as they can determine.

MR. NAUGHTON. If it was not worth anything, it meant nothing, why do you suppose Billie Sol wanted it?

MR. JACKSON. I just don't know.

* * *

MR. SMITH. This statement you put on this balance sheet: Wouldn't you think that a person that was not a CPA would look at that and think that that represented the financial situation?

MR. JACKSON. Well, sir; a person that was not a CPA—like I mentioned a while ago, I am not going to try to say that I used good judgment. Perhaps now—and especially having backsight or hindsight to be able to take advantage of, maybe I did use bad judgment in wording my report.

But certainly at the time I thought I was wording it where anybody would have understood that when I said "no opinion may be expressed" that that would—

MR. SMITH. Then why did you put all the qualification on it? Why didn't you say "This balance sheet shouldn't be taken any stock in," instead of taking all this roundabout wording if you didn't expect it to mislead somebody?

* * *

If this testimony were taken from a trial, the questioners' (prosecutor's) line of argument might be characterized as piercing the veil of the disclaimer. Although an opinion on the statements is disclaimed, a reader of the report might be reasonably entitled to assume that the auditor had done the necessary work with respect to all important items in the balance sheet which were unrelated to inventory. This contention is supported by the pronouncements of the Committee on Auditing Procedure (SAP No. 33, Chapter 10, paragraph 16):

> Whenever the independent auditor disclaims an opinion, he should give *all* substantive reasons for doing so. For example, when he disclaims an opinion because the scope of examination was inadequate, he should also disclose any reservations or exceptions he may have regarding fairness of presentation.

One conclusion that might be drawn is that when a serious limitation on the scope of examination precludes an auditor from forming an opinion on the financial statements taken as a whole, he should elaborate on his inability to form an opinion. In addition to disclosing the restriction on his examination and expressing a disclaimer, he should include a brief statement of the pervasiveness of the disclaimer indicating precisely and in appropriate detail under the circumstances the aspects of the statements on which he cannot form an opinion. This conclusion is supported by a recent decision of the U. S. Court of Appeals for the Fourth Circuit reversing the decision of a U. S. District Court.

The Rhode Island Trust Case. A disclaimer of opinion was involved in a suit by the Rhode Island Hospital Trust National Bank against the accounting firm of Swartz, Bresenoff, Yavner & Jacobs, alleging that the accountants had negligently audited the financial statements of International Trading Corp.[6] The bank made loans to the corporation which the corporation was unable to repay, and the bank sustained a loss in excess of $100,000.

International Trading Corporation, an importer of cement, extended its maximum line of credit at the bank for the purpose of making leasehold improvements to its facilities at Palm Beach, Florida; Brunswick, Georgia; and Providence, Rhode Island. In June 1964, the corporation represented to the bank that during 1963 it had expended $212,000 for this purpose. In fact, the leasehold improvements were totally fictitious, and the labor expenses purportedly incurred for construction of the leasehold improvements were incurred as operating expenses of handling and storing cement.

---

[6] *Rhode Island Hospital Trust National Bank* v. *Swartz, Bresenoff, Yavner & Jacobs,* 455 F. 2d 847 (4th Cir. 1972).

In accordance with the loan agreement establishing the line of credit, the corporation was required to furnish the bank with financial statements for each year, ending December 31. The financial statements for 1963, which were not submitted until June 24, 1964, contained an income statement showing total operating expenses of $610,000 reduced by $212,000 for the cost of leasehold improvements. The balance sheet showed a net worth of $340,000. Thus, the capitalized leasehold improvements represented approximately two-thirds of net assets; and, if the $212,000 had not been capitalized, the income statement would have shown a substantial loss, and the balance sheet would have shown a substantial depletion of net worth.

The report of the auditors accompanying the financial statements was a disclaimer of opinion. The first paragraph stated:

> Our examination included a general review of accounting procedures and such tests of accounting records as we were permitted to make.

Then followed a description of the work that had been performed. For example, they stated that cash in banks had been verified by direct confirmations and reconciled, but that "only 80.98% of the total trade accounts receivable had been confirmed." The concluding paragraph disclaimed an opinion:

> Because of the limitations upon our examination expressed in the preceding paragraphs and the material nature of the items not confirmed directly to us, we are unable to express an opinion as to the fairness of the accompanying statements.

Included in the description of the work performed was a lengthy discussion concerning the crucial leasehold improvements. The critical portion of this passage reads as follows:

> *Additions* to fixed assets in 1963 *were found* to include principally warehouse improvements and installation of machinery and equipment in Providence, Rhode Island, Brunswick, Georgia, and Palm Beach, Florida. Practically *all of this work was done by company employees and materials and overhead was borne by the International Trading Corporation and its affiliates.* Unfortunately, fully complete detailed cost records were not kept of these capital improvements and no exact determination could be made as to the actual cost of said improvements. [Emphasis added by the Court.]

The relative insignificance the court attached to the disclaimer of opinion on the financial statements taken as a whole in comparison with the specific description concerning leasehold improvements is evident in the following excerpt from the decision:

> ...Accountants certified the financial statements, saying overall only that they could not express an opinion with regard to their fairness. This

disclaimer, however, followed other reference to the purported leasehold improvements which expressed no reservation about their existence but only their precise value. We think that a fair reading of Accountant's covering letter and disclaimer indicates that while the leasehold improvements may have had a value of more or less than $212,000.00, there was no question but that they existed and that they had substantial value. Whether Accountants failed to look, or having looked, failed to find, they were guilty of actionable negligence if Bank, in reliance on the statements, made further loans.

In support of this position the court cited several paragraphs in Chapter 10 of SAP No. 33, including paragraph 10, which was quoted and commented upon as follows:

... "The report shall either contain an expression of opinion regarding the financial statements taken as a whole, or an assertion to the effect that an opinion cannot be expressed. *When an overall opinion cannot be expressed, the reasons therefor should be stated ....* " (emphasis added) When Accountants said only that "fully complete detailed cost records were not kept of these capital improvements, and no exact determination could be made as to the actual cost of said improvements," we do not think that the reasons assigned were sufficiently stated. The documentary evidence shows that *no* cost records for material were kept, so that Accountants' statement, viewed even in the most charitable light, was a major understatement, whatever Accountants failed to do.

The appeals court reversed and remanded the decision of the district court—which had been for the accountants—for further proceedings on the issue of the extent of reliance by the bank on the statements in making loans. In addition to the significance of a disclaimer of opinion for legal liability, the court considered two other issues of interest—third-party liability and the importance of the profession's standards. On third-party liability, the court cited *Rusch Factors, Inc.* v. *Levin*, 284 F.S. 85, 93 (D.R.I. 1968) to the effect that "an accountant should be liable in negligence for careless financial misrepresentations relied upon by actually foreseen and limited class of persons." In other words, the decision held that an accountant's liability to third parties for negligence is somewhat broader than that set down in the *Ultramares* case, where such liability was limited to third parties for whose primary benefit financial statements are prepared. The court here held that the accountant's duty of care, and consequent liability for negligence, extends to users of financial statements who, like the plaintiff bank, are actually foreseen by the accountants, though not to the entire class of foreseeable persons. The court's holding in this respect corresponds to the position taken by the American Law Institute in the *Restatement of Torts*, but falls short of extending the liability of accountants for negligence to all foreseeable users of financial statements on which accountants issue their reports.

With respect to the standards of the profession, the court commented as follows:

> Our conclusions with respect to the report and disclosure are reinforced by reference to industry standards of what should have been done in these circumstances. While industry standards may not always be the maximum test of liability, certainly they should be deemed the minimum standards by which liability should be determined. Brief references to American Institute of Certified Public Accountants, *Statements on Auditing Procedure No. 33* (1963) are sufficient to prove the point.

The court then continued to evaluate the shortcomings of the disclaimer of opinion issued by the auditors.

Conclusions

Based on the limited legal precedent in existence on the effect of report language on legal liability, combined with an extrapolation of past cases, the following recommendations are offered:

If the auditor determines that he should issue a qualified opinion, that qualification should be unequivocally expressed. The auditor's qualification should be carefully phrased in words that cannot be later successfully disputed as a mere "explanation" or ignored as not limiting liability in some important respect.

A qualified opinion should be easily distinguishable from the standard short-form report. To express unequivocally the intention to qualify the opinion, not only the words but the *format* of the report should be different enough to identify the type of opinion expressed. In addition, the qualification should identify specific financial statement items, or captions, excepted from the otherwise positive opinion.

No matter what type of report is issued the auditor may at a later date have the burden of establishing that the report issued was appropriate in the circumstances. The courts have attached more significance to the description of the limitations on responsibility in the report than to the *degree* of qualification of the auditor's opinion.

4

Central Reporting Concepts

This chapter presents an overview of reporting concepts that comprise the criteria for deciding the appropriate type of audit report in given circumstances. The discussion is divided between guiding concepts that are general guides to action and directing concepts that are more specific.

Source of Concepts

For the most part, the guiding concepts are logical conclusions based on library research. On the other hand, the directing concepts evolved from studying the details of the case material obtained from the confidential files of public accounting firms and from interviews with practicing independent auditors. Consequently, the directing concepts are inductive generalizations derived from the experience of auditors in the day-to-day application of the fourth standard of reporting.

The role of experience in the development of the directing concepts is extremely important. Practicing auditors, who have been concerned with reporting over a long period of time, have developed views on appropriate reporting criteria. Although this product of experience is frequently unsystematic and not subject to statistical measure, the criteria evolving from practice reflect consideration of a wide range of significant possibilities in reporting circumstances and reflect workable responses to real and difficult problems.

The research process involved giving general names to the criteria used in practice so that these criteria—phrased in terms specific to the decision context in which they were used—could be discussed in general terms. No explicit written account of the report criteria used by auditors—other than the vague guideline of "sufficiently material"— exists in public accounting firm manuals, Institute pronouncements, or widely used auditing textbooks. After the directing concepts were developed, a review of auditing literature, for the most part of the pre-1960 vintage, disclosed fragmented discussion of some of the concepts, and these sources are documented in the discussion when applicable. However, easy identification of these concepts in the literature was possible only after they had been "named" by an inductive analysis of case material.

Guiding Concepts

Guiding concepts in many cases cannot be implemented directly. They are broad guides to action concerned with the general objectives of reporting.

Equity. Diverse groups of people have an interest in audit reports and, in many cases, their goals conflict so that a satisfactory solution to one group may create severe problems for another. Consequently, the writer of an audit report must always consider *equity*—a balancing of the advantages and disadvantages of various forms of audit reports to the several interested groups.

The problems faced by investors when evaluating financial statements for investment purposes must be balanced, for example, against the interests of regulatory agencies interested in using the audit report as a means of social control, and the interests of management in keeping potentially damaging information confidential.

Communication. The preparation of an audit report is essentially a communication process in which the auditor's conclusions about the financial statements are transmitted to the users of the statements. To convey an adequate understanding, the auditor must reduce a complex of judgments to a concise statement, in abstract form, using highly descriptive words. Since users cannot be expected to understand a large number of technical nuances in report language, a high degree of uniformity in the meaning of words used in the report is desirable.

The audit report naturally must be truthful, but the auditor must be concerned with more than literal truth. Since the report is concise, abstract, and—most significantly—one-way, the auditor must be cognizant of the *impression* likely to be drawn by the reader. The communication process permits no dialogue between preparer and user to clarify misimpressions. Consequently, the auditor must be aware that a statement may be literally true, yet create an erroneous impression on the reader.

Environment. The auditor functions within a complex information and regulatory network, and he must be continually aware that he may be held liable for the reliability and understandability of the representations made in his report. This concern with the legal as well as the informational aspect of reports is necessitated by the reporting environment within which the auditor functions. Consideration of the reporting environment is reflected in uniformity of report language and the inclusion of certain information in reports to comply with regulatory agency requirements.

Uniformity. The need for uniformity discussed as an aspect of communication is reinforced by consideration of the reporting environment. Modification of the standard short-form report to implement the fourth reporting standard should be clear and unequivocal. While flexibility versus uniformity in the application of generally accepted accounting principles may continue to be subject to debate, the desirability of uniformity is predominant in the application of the fourth generally accepted auditing standard of reporting.

Regulatory Requirements. The SEC, stock exchanges, and the AICPA all attach considerable importance to the audit report, and over the years these organizations have developed rules and guidelines on reporting. While the influence of report modification on the decision process of investors is indirect and difficult to assess, the influence of report modification on actions taken by the SEC is direct and in many cases dramatic. If the auditor's opinion is not unqualified, the SEC will sometimes halt trading in a company's securities.

The Securities Act of 1933 requires certain companies to file a registration statement with the Commission for each new issue of securities to the public. The Securities Exchange Act of 1934 requires all companies which desire to have their securities listed and registered for public trading on a national stock exchange, and other companies of a certain size, to file a registration application with the Commission and to file annual reports on Form 10-K and certain other periodic reports. The rules of the Commission as expressed in *Regulation S-X* govern the form and content of financial statements and contain a requirement for "certification" of many of these statements by an independent public accountant.

Rule 2-02 contains the Commission's formal requirements as to "certificates," and reads, in part, as follows:

> (c) Opinions to be expressed.—The Accountant's certificate shall state clearly: (i) the opinion of the accountant in respect of the financial statements covered by the certificate and the accounting principles and practices reflected therein; (ii) the opinion of the accountant as to any material changes in accounting principles or practices, or method of applying the accounting principles or practices, or adjustments of the accounts,

required to be set forth by rule 3-07; and (iii) the nature of, and the opinion of the accountant as to, any material differences between the accounting principles and practices reflected in the financial statements and those reflected in the accounts after the entry of adjustments for the periods under review.*

However, under *Regulation S-X,* upon an informal written request by a company, the Commission may allow the omission of the accountant's *opinion* in the "certificate" included in the company's annual report on Form 10-K. In other words, a disclaimer of opinion may be permitted in an annual filing. This waiver of the Commission's rules does not extend to registration statements.

The Commission's administrative policy with respect to other forms of audit reports is found in Accounting Series Releases, which are published opinions of the Chief Accountant on major accounting and administrative questions.

ASR No. 4, issued in 1938, requires *correction* of financial statements based on accounting principles having no substantial authoritative support, or accounting principles which have been formally disapproved by the Commission. For all practical purposes, this means that opinions qualified because of departures from generally accepted accounting principles and adverse opinions are not acceptable to the Commission, and, as far as acceptability to the Commission is concerned, the distinction between an opinion qualified for the above reason and an adverse opinion is unimportant.

ASR No. 90, as explained in Chapter 2, indicates that qualifications or disclaimers based on an inadequate examination are not acceptable to the Commission, but a qualification based on an uncertainty which cannot be resolved at the statement date is acceptable.

In addition to matters of Commission policy concerning qualified opinions, adverse opinions, and disclaimers of opinion, certain Commission regulations relate to disclosures not required for a fair presentation of financial position and results of operations that must be included in unqualified opinions.

Rule 2-02 (c) (iii) of *Regulation S-X,* previously quoted, requires the auditor to disclose in his report any material differences between the accounting principles and practices reflected in the financial statements and those reflected in accounting records, and his opinion on the differences. In practice, these differences are usually disclosed by including an explanatory middle paragraph between the conventional scope and opinion paragraphs. For example, a company which,

---

* On June 23, 1972, Regulation S-X was amended by Securities Act of 1933, Release No. 5261, to effectively remove the provision in Rule 2-02 (c) (iii).

for some reason, keeps its books and files its tax returns on a cash basis could prepare financial statements on an accrual basis, and the auditor could express an unqualified opinion on the conformity of the statements with generally accepted accounting principles. The difference between the records and statements would be disclosed in an explanatory middle paragraph of the audit report.

An explanatory middle paragraph disclosure is also required by ASR No. 13, issued in 1940, when the audited company's accounting system has major inadequacies. ASR No. 13 deals with an examination in which the auditor was forced to make extensive adjustments of the accounts. The last paragraph of ASR No. 13 summarizes the view of the Chief Accountant on the matter:

> In my opinion, when a registrant during the period under review has not maintained records adequate for the purpose of preparing comprehensive and dependable financial statements, that fact should be disclosed. If, because of the absence or gross inadequacy of accounting records maintained by a registrant, it is necessary to have essential books of account prepared retroactively and for the accountant to enlarge the scope of the audit to the extent indicated in order to be able to express his opinion, these facts also should be disclosed, and I believe it is misleading, notwithstanding partial disclosure by footnotes as in the instant case, to furnish a certificate which implies that the accountant was satisfied to express an opinion based on a test-check audit. Moreover, it is misleading, in my opinion, to state or imply that accepted principles of accounting have been consistently followed by a registrant during the period under review, if in fact during such period books of account were not maintained by a registrant or were grossly inadequate, or if it has been necessary for the accountant to make pervasive and extraordinary adjustments of the character under consideration.

In summary, an auditor should be aware of the administrative position of a regulatory agency concerning the acceptability of the various forms of reports other than unqualified opinions and, in some cases, may need to modify even an unqualified opinion in response to agency requirements.

Directing Concepts

While the guiding concepts are goals to seek in the preparation of audit reports, directing concepts offer more specific guidance for making the decision of what type of audit report is appropriate in given circumstances. Not all of the directing concepts are relevant to every reporting decision, and no single directing concept is conclusive in the decision process. The purpose of this discussion is to provide a general exposition of all factors to be considered in the reporting decision. The relevance of directing concepts to specific reporting problems and circumstances, and recommendations concerning the incorporation of the concepts in pronouncements of the Committee on Auditing Procedure are discussed in later chapters.

In the present literature on reporting, the sole criterion suggested for determining whether a qualified opinion, an adverse opinion, or disclaimer of opinion is appropriate is the degree of materiality of the cause of the exception. The following excerpts from Chapter 10 of SAP No. 33 illustrate the typical reference to materiality:

Unusual Uncertainties as to the Effect of
Future Developments on Certain Items

47. In some instances where the outcome of a matter is uncertain, the amount concerned may be *so material* that a qualified opinion is inappropriate. [Emphasis added.]

Adverse Opinion

13. An adverse opinion is required in any report where the exceptions as to fairness of presentation are *so material* that in the independent auditor's judgment a qualified opinion is not justified. . . . [Emphasis added.]

The measurement of degree of materiality which comes most readily to mind is relative *magnitude,* such as percentage of total assets. However, materiality is basically a measure of relative *importance,* which is not entirely dependent on relative size. Materiality has both quantitative and qualitative characteristics; one classification of this dual aspect is found in a report of the 1954 Committee on Accounting Concepts and Standards of the American Accounting Association:

1. Characteristics having primarily quantitative significance:
    a. The magnitude of the item (either smaller or larger) relative to normal expectation.
    b. The magnitude of the item relative to similar or related items (relative to the total of its class, earnings for the period, etc.).
2. Characteristics having primarily qualitative significance:
    a. The inherent importance of the action, activity, or condition reflected (unusual, unexpected, improper, in violation of contract or statute, etc.).
    b. The inherent importance of the item as an indicator of the probable course of future events (suggestive of a change in business practice, etc.).[1]

The major overriding conclusion drawn from the study of the decision-making criteria used by auditors for audit reports is that materiality—as it relates to the type-of-report decision—is a matter

---

[1] *Accounting and Reporting Standards for Corporate Financial Statements and Preceding Statements and Supplements,* American Accounting Association, 1957, p. 49.

primarily of qualitative importance. In addition, the qualitative characteristics considered are far more extensive than "inherent importance" as described in the AAA committee report.

In outline form, the directing concepts are (in order of consideration rather than importance):

I.   Relative magnitude (size test).

II. Probability (the acceptable level of uncertainty inherent in statement preparation).
    A.   Uncertainty of outcome.
       1.   Imminence of resolution.
       2.   Sufficiency of past experience.
    B.   Likelihood of error.

III. Utility (financial statement analysis).
    A.   Expertise.
    B.   Pervasiveness.
    C.   Nature of item (inherent importance).

Relative Magnitude. The dollar impact of an item on the financial statements is the usual meaning associated with materiality. In this respect, the reporting concept of relative magnitude does not differ from the typical concern with materiality in accounting. In this context, materiality is a measure of relative significance which is determined by comparing the amount of the item of interest to some relevant basis of comparison, such as net income for the period, normal net income, or total current assets. For many years accounting authorities have used "material" to qualify expressions of opinions or positions. Accounting Principles Board Opinions, Statements on Auditing Procedure, and Releases of the SEC are all replete with references to the term.

This monograph does not offer any quantitative guidelines for determining what is *material* per se. The main question of interest for the type-of-report decision is concerned with the step from an exception that is material, to one that is *sufficiently* material to make a *qualified* opinion unjustified. The initial determination that an exception is material enough to make an *unqualified* opinion unjustified does not differ significantly from the type of evaluation contemplated in the typical reference to materiality in accounting literature. On the other hand, determination that an exception is "sufficiently material" is a problem unique to the type-of-report decision. In other words, this monograph is concerned with the distinction between material and sufficiently material rather than the distinction between material and immaterial.

The basic determination of material versus immaterial is neither a settled nor a trivial problem in accounting; however, the topic has received more than limited attention from other researchers and is the subject of an accounting research study of the Institute's accounting research division.[2]   Consequently, the limited attention devoted to the subject in this monograph seems justified.

In the decision-making process of determining what type of audit report is appropriate, the material/immaterial decision is the first step. Once an exception is evaluated as material, the other reporting concepts are used to determine whether report modification should be limited to qualification of the opinion.

Auditors commonly evaluate materiality on the basis of how the amount of the item in question affects the significance of common analytic relationships. Departures from generally accepted accounting principles are frequently evaluated in terms of profitability relationships, such as impact on average earnings, the stability of earnings, and growth of earnings. On the other hand, uncertainties are normally evaluated in terms of liquidity measures, such as the adequacy of working capital and measures of the ability to meet fixed obligations. Beyond this method of analysis, auditors do not consistently use any widely accepted relative magnitude cut-off points for the reporting decision.

Documentation of materiality evaluations in Institute pronouncements is rare. However, in SAP No. 2 (1939) the Committee on Auditing Procedure considered a case involving a restricted examination in which the auditor did not audit the branch offices of a client company. The facts of the case were as follows:

> The circumstances surrounding the particular engagement, as furnished to the committee, are as follows: Approximately 50 per cent of a client's assets are represented by current assets. Inventories account for 55 per cent of the current assets, and receivables an additional 13 per cent. Over 90 per cent of the receivables are maintained at branch offices and approximately 60 per cent of the inventories are located at branches. Approximately 90 per cent of sales (and thus presumably 90 per cent of the income) originate at the branches. The cash and fixed-asset accounts, investments and other asset accounts can be

---

[2]   For examples of empirical research on materiality, see: Samuel Mitchell Woolsey, "Criteria for Judging Materiality in Accounting in Certain Selected Situations" (unpublished dissertation, University of Texas at Austin, 1954); Leopold A. Bernstein, "The Concept of Materiality," *The Accounting Review*, January 1967, pp. 86-95; Fred Neumann, "The Auditing Standard of Consistency," *Empirical Research in Accounting: Selected Studies, 1968,* Supplement to Vol. 6, *Journal of Accounting Research,* pp. 1-17; and Paul Frishkoff, "An Empirical Investigation of Materiality in Accounting," *Empirical Research in Accounting: Selected Studies, 1970,* supplement to Vol. 8, *Journal of Accounting Research,* pp. 116-129.

satisfactorily examined at the head office. Most of the liabilities originate at the branches. The branch accounts are examined by the client's internal auditing staff.

The committee is also informed that the company is well managed, its accounts are conservatively stated and there is no reason, from the work done at head office, to question the completeness and accuracy of the reports of the traveling auditors.

The committee concluded that an opinion should not be expressed. They stated:

> In view of the materiality of the assets and transactions involved, the committee is of the opinion that in this case the exceptions with regard to the scope of the examination are sufficiently material to negative the expression of an opinion, and that, accordingly, the auditors should refrain from expressing one.

The assets not examined constituted approximately 22 per cent of total assets and 45 per cent of current assets. However, these assets accounted for approximately 90 per cent of revenue and, "presumably," 90 per cent of earnings. Since the committee could have recommended a disclaimer of opinion on the income statement and a qualified opinion on the balance sheet, an easy conclusion would be that the percentages involved indicate amounts that are *sufficiently* material. However, while 22 per cent of total assets and 45 per cent of current assets are certainly material, their relative magnitude does not seem overwhelming when the amounts are viewed as maximum potential misstatements. The percentages would be evaluated at that level only if the assets were completely fictitious. A more reasonable conclusion is that other factors, not enumerated, influenced the committee's judgment. This conclusion would be compatible with the decision-making criteria used by auditors today.

The difficulty of explaining all the factors which influence the reporting decision was probably an important reason for the failure to include the contents of SAP No. 2 and other SAPs dealing with reporting on restricted examinations in the *Codification of Statements on Auditing Procedure* (1951). The considerations in addition to relative magnitude which are important are discussed in the following reporting concepts.

Probability. Audited financial statements can never be completely accurate. The accounting process leading to the preparation of financial statements and the audit process leading to the expression of an opinion on the statements are both susceptible to error, as is any process that must depend on human judgment and volition. However, the probability of error is at an acceptable, or at least accepted, level in normal circumstances.

Both financial-statement preparation and auditing have standards of quality against which they are measured. For auditing, generally accepted auditing standards are the measure of quality. Two sets of standards are applicable to financial statement preparation: the process of selection and accumulation of data for financial statements is evaluated in terms of an effective system of internal control. The propriety of financial statement presentation is evaluated in terms of conformity with generally accepted accounting principles. The probability of error when these standards of quality have been met defines the acceptable probability of error in audited financial statements.

The reporting concept of "probability" is particularly relevant to two problem areas of reporting: (1) unusual uncertainties which cannot be reasonably estimated or otherwise satisfactorily resolved and (2) limitations on the scope of the examination. These problems are evaluated in terms of "uncertainty of outcome" and "likelihood of error," respectively.

Uncertainty of Outcome. When an exception relates to (1) the outcome of an event which depends on future developments or on a future decision by parties other than management or (2) the valuation of assets when realization is not reasonably determinable, an evaluation of the *degree of uncertainty* is necessary. In fact, without consideration of the probable outcome of unresolved matters, even the relative magnitude of the matter cannot be assessed. The potential relative magnitude must be combined with an evaluation of probability to determine an expected relative magnitude before the usual evaluation of quantitative materiality can be made.

The importance of uncertainty of outcome was considered by Carman Blough in relation to the problem of auditing "small business investment companies" (SBIC).[3] The principal asset of a SBIC is its investment in small, high-risk companies. Usually the auditor of an SBIC has enough reservations about the fairness of the valuation at which these investments are carried to require a qualified opinion. According to Mr. Blough, in some situations even a qualified opinion would not be justified.

> However, this would not be proper where the range of uncertainty is so great that it is unreasonable to give credibility to the representations.[4]

---

[3] Carman G. Blough, "Some SBIC Audit Problems," *The Journal of Accountancy*, March 1963, pp. 71-72.
[4] *Ibid.,* p. 71.

Evidently when the range of uncertainty is great enough, a disclaimer of opinion is called for. In his evaluation of uncertainty, two factors are of primary concern to the auditor—(1) imminence and (2) experience.

The *imminence* of an event relates to how soon in point of time the resolution of the event will have an impact on the financial statements. For example, if a company is engaged in protracted litigation which is likely to be drawn out over a ten-year period, the imminence of the impact on the statements is far removed, and the need to disclaim an opinion is highly unlikely. The distance of the event on the time horizon lowers the expected relative magnitude of the event in relation to the current financial statements and also allows the company to plan to increase its ability to absorb the impact of the event if it is adverse.

The role of *experience* in the evaluation of uncertainty concerns the auditor's ability to relate the reasonableness of judgment about the future to the company's past activities. If there is a backlog of experience relevant to the event under consideration, very often a reasonable estimate of the outcome is possible by an extrapolation of past experience. On the other hand, without relevant past experience, greater uncertainty is inherent in the event.

Likelihood of Error. When an exception relates to the failure to apply normal, or customary, auditing procedures to a portion of the financial statements, an evaluation of the likelihood of error is necessary. In applying this reporting criterion, the auditor attempts to determine the relative magnitude of the potential misstatement that may remain undetected because of failure to apply certain auditing procedures.

The criterion of likelihood of error was suggested by the Committee on Auditing Procedure in its consideration of the problem of reporting on interim financial statements. In determining whether the omission of certain auditing procedures should preclude the expression of an opinion, it suggested the auditor should consider the likelihood of error in the financial statements:

> The test in this connection should be whether the exceptions as to the scope of the examination concern items which could easily be incorrect and which if incorrect are of such importance that the position and results could be misstated to a significant extent. For example, an exception that minor bank balances had not been confirmed would not be of sufficient importance to negative the opinion; an exception that intervening property additions had not been vouched might similarly be unimportant if these were of minor amounts. But an exception to the effect that the auditor had gone to the head office only and had not visited numerous branches at which he would normally make an examination probably would negative the opinion, as also

would an exception that the auditor had made no examination of the inventories, either as to the book records or the physical inventories themselves; and the committee believes that in such circumstances no opinion should be expressed.[5]

A close analysis of the committee's expressed view reveals a concern with the importance of the items not examined to financial position and results of operations. In other words, a consideration of the likelihood of error must be combined with a consideration of reporting utility.

Utility. When he believes an exception is necessary, an auditor must decide whether his conclusions concerning the financial statements can be adequately expressed by a qualified opinion. In reaching this decision, the auditor must consider the usefulness of the financial statements when read in conjunction with the audit report.

The concept of utility is the single most important reporting guideline. Once the relative magnitude of an exception has been assessed, attention must be turned to the several factors that are pertinent to financial statement utility from a reporting standpoint.

General. Although the reporting concept of utility has not been suggested in Institute pronouncements on reporting, other Institute literature prepared to interpret the pronouncements has referred to its importance. For example, an article by Carman Blough contained the following statement:

> ...If the CPA's exceptions as to the company's accounting practices, or limitations on the scope of his audit, would require him to so qualify his opinion as to make it valueless to the readers of his report, he should refrain from expressing any opinion at all.[6]

Another reference appears in a pamphlet prepared by the Institute research staff to explain the meaning of the auditor's report.

> In general, the necessity for expressing a qualified opinion occurs when the CPA has not been able to make an examination sufficiently complete to warrant the expression of an unqualified opinion or when he has found violations of accepted accounting principles which the company is unwilling to correct. When either of these situations exists, the CPA weighs their significance and importance. *If the statements read in the light of his*

---

[5] Statement on Auditing Procedure No. 8, "Interim Financial Statements and the Auditor's Report Thereon," American Institute of Accountants, New York, September 1941, p. 57.

[6] Carman G. Blough, "Significance of Auditing Statement No. 23," *The Journal of Accountancy*, March 1951, p. 393. Naturally, under present reporting standards, exceptions to accounting practices would lead to an adverse opinion.

qualifications permit a reasonable appraisal of the financial position and results of operations, he expresses a qualified opinion.[7] [Emphasis added.]

The task of assessing the utility of financial statements, when viewed from a broad perspective, is an imposing challenge—one that raises questions that border on the unanswerable. Useful to whom, and for what purpose? In the audit reporting context, however, consideration of utility is a much narrower and, therefore, less burdensome undertaking.

The alternative courses of action to be taken as a result of the assessment of utility are highly circumscribed. The auditor's choice may involve a simple dichotomy—a qualified opinion versus a disclaimer of opinion or adverse opinion. If the audit report adequately conveys the auditor's conclusions concerning the fair presentation of the financial statements, reporting utility is achieved. In addition, auditors typically evaluate utility with respect to certain specific elements. The evaluation is not open-ended. Utility—as an audit reporting concept—has three relevant elements: (1) the expertise of the auditor in relation to the exception, (2) the pervasiveness of the exception, and (3) the nature of the item which is the subject of the exception.

Expertise. Early recognition of the important role of "expertise" in reporting is found in ASR No. 7, issued over thirty years ago, in which two among several deficiencies cited in audit reports were:

> Disclaimer of responsibility on the part of the certifying accountants with respect to matters clearly within their province.
>
> Reservations on the part of the certifying accountants with respect to matters not within their province which might indicate that apparently the accountants were not satisfied that such matters as legal titles, outstanding liabilities, etc., were properly reflected in the financial statements.[8]

The first paragraph quoted indicates that the auditor should accept responsibility for the fair presentation of a financial statement item if the type of evaluation required is within his competence. The second paragraph indicates that some aspects of financial statement presentation may not be within the auditor's competence and that he should not comment on these matters unless he has some reason to believe they are not fairly presented.

Underlying the quoted assertions from ASR No. 7 is the thought that financial statement users have certain reasonable expectations

---

7 "Audits by Certified Public Accountants," American Institute of Accountants, New York, 1950, p. 19.

8 "Commonly Cited Deficiencies in Financial Statements Filed Under the Securities Act of 1933 and the Securities Exchange Act of 1934," Accounting Series Release No. 7, Securities and Exchange Commission, Washington, D.C., 1938.

about the type of responsibility assumed by the auditor in expressing an opinion on financial statements. This reasonable understanding of the auditor's responsibility does not change unless the audit report is modified to indicate a different responsibility, as is the case in qualified opinions, adverse opinions, or disclaimers of opinion. However, if evaluation of a financial statement item is clearly within the auditor's competence, a modification of the report which avoids responsibility for an opinion on the item is not appropriate.

If the audit report indicates that the auditor is declining responsibility for an item, the report user then has the burden of making the evaluation the auditor has declined. ASR No. 7 indicates in general terms the type of responsibility the auditor may not appropriately decline. One specific example of this type of responsibility is evaluation of the adequacy of the auditor's examination. In an article interpreting an Institute pronouncement on reporting, Carman Blough had this to say:

> ...Third parties, since they lack the facilities to make such an appraisal, should not be required to evaluate the work done by the CPA.[9]

In a later discussion concerning a more specific aspect of restricted scope, Mr. Blough reiterated this view:

> ...If the auditor substitutes other procedures for satisfying himself with respect to the fairness of the amount of the inventory in place of the observation of the taking of the inventory he must decide either that he has sufficient grounds for an unqualified opinion or that he does not have sufficient grounds for any opinion. In our opinion, he has no right to shift to the reader of the report the burden of determining the possible importance of an inadequate examination.[10]

Thus, if a matter falls within the auditor's expertise, he should assume responsibility for its evaluation; he may not appropriately shift that responsibility to report users.

When applied to typical exceptions found in audit reports, the inherent soundness of the reporting criterion of expertise is apparent. If the auditor feels that an accounting practice followed by a company is questionable, he must determine whether the practice is a departure from generally accepted accounting principles. The auditor may not merely call attention to the practice by using phrases in his report such as "fairly present when read in conjunction with footnote X," when the footnote describes an accounting practice of the company.

---

[9] Blough, "Significance of Auditing Statement No. 23," page 391.
[10] Carman G. Blough, "SEC Release on Opinions and Opening Inventories," *The Journal of Accountancy*, May 1962, p. 72.

In similar fashion, the auditor must evaluate the impact of inadequacies in his examination on the statements. The need to evaluate whether *any* opinion may be expressed has been mentioned. In addition, even if the auditor determines that a qualified opinion is appropriate, the qualification must be based on the impact of the exception on the financial statements. The importance of the scope limitation should not be a matter the report reader has to evaluate. For example, a qualifying phrase such as "except for the above-mentioned limitation on the scope of our examination" is not acceptable.

The most significant impact on reporting of the "expertise" criterion is in the area of qualifications or disclaimers of opinion based on unusual uncertainties. In these cases, the cause of the exception should be a matter that is not within the expertise of the auditor—the type of matter that a reader of the report should not reasonably expect the auditor to be able to evaluate. For example, some accountants have suggested that an exception concerning a current asset should never lead to an opinion qualified "subject to" an uncertainty. Although, for example, uncertainties are involved in the collection of receivables, allowing for uncollectible accounts is an estimate inherent in the accounting process and, consequently, a matter of accounting expertise. They reason that if the auditor questions the adequacy of the allowance his opinion should be qualified by an "except for" phrase indicating a departure from the generally accepted accounting principle of pre-senting accounts receivable at estimated collection value.

On the other hand, although the auditor ordinarily should be able to form a definite opinion on the fair presentation of current assets, the critical element is not the asset classification, but the relevance of the auditor's expertise. Usually the auditor's expertise is relevant in making estimates of the valuation of current assets, but sometimes the estimate involves factors outside his competence. Consequently, not all exceptions concerning current assets are accurately described as departures from generally accepted accounting principles.

Pervasiveness. A reporting criterion of major importance is pervasiveness. If the cause of the report exception is so *pervasive* that it permeates the financial statements and makes appraisal of the statements virtually impossible, a qualified opinion is not justified. Conversely, if the exception can be isolated and the auditor can report rather precisely the significance of the exception for the financial statements, a qualified opinion is possible.

In relation to exceptions to fair presentation, Carman Blough expressed the criterion of pervasiveness, or isolability, as follows:

> ...In some cases where the departure from generally accepted accounting principles is not so complex, and where the auditor can report precisely its

significance with respect to the financial statements presented, it may be possible to explain the situation and express a qualified opinion.[11]

The pervasiveness criterion is also endorsed by another writer, who indicates that departures from generally accepted accounting principles should not lead to qualified opinions in the following circumstances:

> ...The existence of infractions of generally accepted accounting principles ... *are so many or so complex that no clear picture is presented.*[12] [Emphasis added.]
>
> ...When the effect of failure to follow generally accepted accounting principles cannot be expressed in the accountant's report in such a manner that the financial position and operating results can reasonably be determined by the reader.[13]

One case discussed by Mr. Blough offers an example of an exception to fair presentation that is *isolable* and illustrates the relation of pervasiveness to the more fundamental reporting concept of utility. The client company proposed presenting a balance sheet in which the capital stock of $100,000 and the retained earnings of $1,000,000 were combined and reported in one figure. Mr. Blough advised the CPA writing the report that the proposed presentation did require an exception, but that a qualified opinion was justified.

> ...It seems to us there is enough importance in knowing that the assets and liabilities are fairly stated to make it worth issuing a balance sheet even though the proprietorship section is inadequate. We believe a CPA would be justified in expressing a qualified opinion on such a statement because, while insufficient, it is not misleading.[14]

The reporting criterion of pervasiveness is also an important indicator of whether a disclaimer of opinion is necessary when the exception relates to an unusual uncertainty. The following excerpt from one of the few non-Institute publications on reporting illustrates the evaluation of whether an uncertainty permeates the statements.

> Where matters over which neither the auditor nor the company has control are such that they may be expected to change the statements at a number of basic points, a disclaimer seems to be a logical treatment. Such a situation would exist when the selling price of a large part of the product sold during the year had not been determined. Not only would earned surplus be

---

[11] Carman G. Blough, *Practical Applications of Accounting Standards*, AICPA, New York, 1957, pp. 159-160.

[12] Jennie M. Palen, *Report Writing for Accountants*, Prentice-Hall, Inc., Englewood Cliffs, N.J., 1955, p. 399.

[13] Ibid., p. 408.

[14] Blough, *Practical Applications*, p. 156.

meaningless, but the income statement would require later revision all the way back to the sales figures.[15]

The same source also indicates that a qualified opinion is not appropriate if the exception cannot be isolated for the report reader's evaluation:

> If the auditor is able to express an opinion on the financial statements except so far as they may be affected by some contingency whose outcome neither he nor the company can determine, he should make clear disclosure of the contingency and express a qualified opinion, *unless* the uncertainties are *so all-embracing* he prefers to disclaim one.[16] [Emphasis added.]

The reporting criteria grouped under the heading of "utility" are interrelated, and uncertainties which are so *all-embracing* that they require a disclaimer may be indicated by the nature of the item causing the exception.

Nature of Item. Most basic in consideration of the nature of an item is whether the exception relates to a specific matter or a general condition. The former is an appropriate matter for qualification, while the latter cannot be adequately described by a qualified opinion.

A qualified opinion is justified when the report reader can identify the circumstances giving rise to the qualification and may, appropriately, make his own evaluation of the exception. In other words, the qualification directs the reader's attention to a localized problem area—an isolated and specific exception.

On the other hand, if the exception relates to a general condition, the report reader is unable to determine clearly how and to what extent the financial statements may not be fairly presented.

An example of a specific exception would be a qualification with respect to the realization of a particular asset. In contrast, doubt about whether the company is a going concern is a general condition which permeates the statements.

The nature of the item is less basic, but also merits concern, in assessing the importance of relative magnitude. For example, Carman Blough offered the following suggestion for determining the materiality of an item:

> As to what percentages one might use as criteria, we feel the particular facts have considerable effect. For example, we believe that the percentage should be higher before excluding a loss growing out of the sale of a piece of depreciable property previously used in the business than would be true in the

---

[15] Palen, *Report Writing*, pp. 408-409.

[16] *Ibid.*, p. 377. Naturally, the decision to disclaim an opinion should not be a matter of *preference*, but a *determination* of what report is appropriate in the circumstances.

case of the write-off of a material amount of intangibles or a credit from the elimination of an unused reserve. Reasons for this distinction are (1) the management's discretion as to the year in which the item is to be recognized and (2) the degree of relationship to operations.[17]

Thus, the reporting concept of "nature of item" brings us full circle to a consideration of relative magnitude and the importance of the item in the report reader's decision-making process. In this latter context, however, the nature of the item has a greater bearing on the material/immaterial distinction than on the material/sufficiently material distinction.

Summary

The reporting concepts encompassed within the criterion of "sufficiently material" are diverse and far reaching. In fact, "sufficiently material" encompasses so many other criteria that classifying the type-of-report decision as one among many considerations of *materiality* seems to be an oversimplification.

The guiding reporting concepts are general objectives of audit report writing and consist of (1) equity, (2) communication, and (3) awareness of the reporting environment. The directing reporting concepts, in contrast to the guiding concepts, are more specific guides to the report-type decision and consist of (1) relative magnitude, (2) probability, and, most important, (3) utility. Only the first of these—relative magnitude—has received widespread attention in discussions of materiality.

The extremely important reporting concept of utility normally leads to an evaluation of three aspects of the usefulness to financial statement readers of the audit report combined with the financial statements: (1) expertise of the auditor in relation to the financial statement item causing the report exception, (2) the pervasiveness of the exception, and (3) the nature of the financial statement item which is the source of the exception.

---

[17] Carman G. Blough, "Some Suggested Criteria for Determining 'Materiality'," *The Journal of Accountancy*, April 1950, p. 354.

5

Exceptions Based on Uncertainty

Periodic financial reporting is necessitated by the demand for useful and timely financial information in a dynamic economy. This demand necessitates many estimates and judgments in the process of financial statement preparation, and financial reports covering short periods of time must be tentative. However, if financial information is too tentative, financial statements will not be useful. Consequently, in forming his opinion on the statements the auditor must evaluate the degree of uncertainty which attaches to the financial statements.

Present Reporting Criteria

Present reporting criteria for dealing with financial statement uncertainties are enumerated in Chapter 10 of SAP No. 33 as follows:

Unusual Uncertainties as to the Effect of
Future Developments on Certain Items

45. The management of a company ordinarily is expected to evaluate matters affecting financial position and results of operations. In cases where the probable effects of a matter are not reasonably determinable at the time of the opinion, such as in the case of certain lawsuits, tax matters, and other contingencies which may have a material effect upon the financial statements, and the final outcome is dependent upon the decision of parties other than management, the independent auditor should appropriately qualify his opinion. In such instances use of the phrase "subject to" is appropriate. . . .

46. Occasionally, uncertainties arising from questions of valuation or realizability of assets dependent upon management's judgment may require a qualification of opinion. In such cases, use of the phrase "subject to" is also considered appropriate. . . .

47. In some instances where the outcome of a matter is uncertain, the amount concerned may be so material that a qualified opinion is inappropriate. An example of such a situation would be a case in which the company

is a defendant in a suit claiming damages of a very large amount in relation to the company's net assets and there is considerable uncertainty as to the outcome of the suit. In such cases, the facts may be disclosed in a middle paragraph of the independent auditor's report and the disclaimer of opinion. . . .

As the heading for the subject in SAP No. 33 indicates, the auditor should take exception in his report only for *unusual* uncertainties. These uncertainties are primarily matters which depend on future developments or on a future decision by parties other than management. However, an unusual uncertainty may also arise in connection with the valuation of an asset, which normally involves a judgment by management rather than a decision by an outside party. Situations of this nature must be carefully distinguished from those in which the auditor definitely disagrees with the valuation of a financial statement item. In addition, since many uncertainties are involved in financial statement preparation, clarification of an *unusual* uncertainty is essential.

Clarification is also needed for semantical confusion that sometimes occurs when auditors talk about exceptions based on uncertainty. When an uncertainty cannot be resolved by the report date, the auditor is unable to form an opinion on the fairness of an item in the financial statements. Since another way of saying this is that the auditor has not been able to obtain sufficient competent evidential matter about an item, an uncertainty exception is sometimes referred to as a scope limitation. On the other hand, because of the major heading classifications used in Chapter 10 of SAP No. 33, these qualifications are also referred to as exceptions to fair presentation. The category of reports involving unusual uncertainties is unique and important enough to require separate identification and should not be aggregated with either scope limitations or exceptions to fairness. Uncertainty exceptions should not be described as scope limitations since the latter term more appropriately describes situations in which the auditor has not carried out audit procedures he considers necessary. For uncertainty exceptions, the auditor cannot apply any audit procedures to obtain satisfaction. On the other hand, exceptions to fair presentation more appropriately apply to an intentional matter of presentation—failure to disclose adequate information, failure to adhere to generally accepted accounting principles, or inconsistent application of accounting principles.

Nature of Unusual Uncertainties

The nature and complexity of the economic activity which financial statements attempt to reflect preclude exact measurement. While economic activity is continuous, financial statements are prepared at specified intervals of time. Accounting measurements made in financial statement preparation require the allocation of the results of complex activities among relatively short periods of time, and the process necessitates many estimates, approximations, and judgments.

Assets represent costs to be allocated to future periods in anticipation of future benefits. Eventual benefits will not necessarily equal the expected ones. Liabilities are subject to a similar sort of uncertainty to the extent that they represent anticipated obligations of past events.

In the preparation of financial statements, these estimates, approximations, and judgments are initially made by management. The function served by the auditor is to appraise these decisions by management with a detached interest: are the judgments reasonable from the viewpoint of an impartial observer?

Since no present evidence exists of the future on which the validity of these judgments depends, the decisions must be guided by what has happened in the past. This assessment of what will happen in the future based on past experience has similarities to the process of inductive reasoning—an attempt to attach some measure of conclusiveness to an argument. According to a classic work on probability:

> . . .the validity of every induction, strictly interpreted, depends, not on a matter of fact, but on the existence of a relation of probability. An inductive argument affirms, not that a certain matter of fact *is* so, but that *relative to certain evidence* there is a probability in its favor. The validity of the induction, relative to the original evidence, is not upset, therefore, if, as a fact, the truth turns out to be otherwise.
>
> The clear apprehension of this truth profoundly modifies our attitude towards the solution of the inductive problem. The validity of the inductive method does *not* depend on the success of its predictions. Its repeated failure in the past may, of course, supply us with new evidence, the inclusion of which will modify the force of subsequent inductions. But the force of the old induction *relative to the old evidence* is untouched. The evidence with which our experience has supplied us in the past may have proved misleading, but this is entirely irrelevant to the question of what conclusions we ought reasonably to have drawn from the evidence then before us.[1]

The auditor must evaluate the uncertainty which attaches to the accounting measurements made in the preparation of financial statements. He does so by a process of induction, relating past experience to the judgments of management concerning the future. By their very nature the estimates, approximations, and judgments made in financial statement preparation cannot be accurate—in the sense that what is expected will actually come about. The auditor can only conclude either

---

[1] J. M. Keynes, *A Treatise on Probability*, Macmillan, London, 1921 (1948 ed.), p. 221.

that the judgments are reasonable or unreasonable in the light of past experience or that he cannot form a judgment.

An uncertainty is unusual if the probability of the outcome of an event as judged by management is in the auditor's view abnormal in relation to the evidence of past events of a similar nature. In this sense, "probability" refers to rational rather than statistical probability. In his classic work on probability, Keynes discusses rational (nonnumeric) probability as follows:

> There is a vagueness, it may be noticed, in the number of instances, which would be required. . .to establish a given numerical degree of probability, which corresponds to the vagueness in the degree of probability which we do actually attach to inductive conclusions. We assume that the necessary number of instances is finite, but we do not know what the number is. We know that the probability of a well-established induction is great, but, when we are asked to name its degree, we cannot. Common sense tells us that some inductive arguments are stronger than others, and that some are very strong. But how much stronger or how strong we cannot express. The probability of an induction is only numerically definite when we are able to make definite assumptions about the number of independent equiprobable influences at work. Otherwise, it is nonnumerical, though bearing relations of greater and less to numerical probabilities according to the approximate limits within which our assumption as to the possible number of these causes lies.[2]

An auditor's evaluation of uncertainty is a formation of judgment on the degree of rational belief and not a conclusion concerning numeric probability.

Starting from the proposition that an auditor evaluates financial statement uncertainties by judging the reasonableness of management's view of the future in the light of past experience, unusual uncertainties may be distinguished as those involving judgments in which the link to past experience is very unclear or nonexistent. For example, uncertainties relating to the realization of assets (collectibility of accounts receivable) are resolved by *economic* events subsequent to the date of the financial statements. Exact prediction of these subsequent economic events is not possible, but, normally, a history of prior economic events similar to economic events of the future can be used as a sound basis for judging the reasonableness of management's decisions concerning realization. These estimates are inherent in the accounting process, the link to past experience is well-established, and the uncertainties are not unusual.

On the other hand, resolution of some uncertainties is not attributable to general economic events occurring subsequent to the

---

[2] *Ibid.*, p. 259.

date of financial statements, but rather to some future specific events. These events are unique and have no well-established link to past experience. For example, renegotiation proceedings, utility revenue rate cases, and litigation of claims for damages are resolved by processes outside the market place, and past experience may be either nonexistent or an unreliable guide to eventual settlement. These matters are *unusual* uncertainties.

In between these two extremes are uncertainties relating to the realization of assets for which past experience is an inadequate guide, even though the uncertainty will be resolved by subsequent economic events. For example, some research and development costs involving the creation of new products cannot be evaluated in the light of past experience because the products are unlike any marketed in the past. These uncertainties are appropriately regarded as unusual.

Application of Reporting Concepts

Most of the directing reporting concepts are relevant to the evaluation of exceptions based on uncertainty. However, some concepts are far more important than others.

Relative Magnitude. By its very nature, the relative magnitude of an uncertainty cannot be presumptive in determining whether a disclaimer of opinion or a qualified opinion is appropriate. If realization of an asset or the outcome of a matter such as litigation is uncertain, the effect on the financial statements can only be *potentially* significant. The total potential adjustment to the statements must be combined with an evaluation of probability.

Probability. In evaluating the probability of uncertainties, the auditor must first estimate the dollar effect on the financial statements of the various possible outcomes of the uncertainty. A dollar amount can normally be attached to the most favorable outcome and the most adverse outcome. Between these two extremes may be several discrete possibilities. The next step in the evaluation is a judgment concerning the likelihood of each outcome. This does not mean that a numeric probability must be attached to each possible outcome; most frequently, the evaluation will be in terms of qualitative likelihood, such as good, average, or poor. Finally, the dollar magnitude of all outcomes with a better than average chance of occurrence may be compared with the normal bases of comparison in the financial statements in the determination of relative magnitude.

The dollar amounts included for the uncertainty in the comparison should be reasonably conservative. As Keynes notes:

> All propositions are true or false, but the knowledge we have of them depends on our circumstances; and while it is often convenient to speak of propositions as certain or probable, this expresses strictly a relationship in which they stand to a *corpus* of knowledge, actual or hypothetical, and not a characteristic of the propositions in themselves. A proposition is capable at the same time of varying degrees of this relationship, depending upon the knowledge to which it is related, so that it is without significance to call a proposition probable unless we specify the knowledge to which we are relating it.[3]

Keynes' discussion has two relevant observations. Although the auditor evaluates the relative likelihood of various possible outcomes, the entity will experience only one outcome—hence the need for conservatism. Also, the auditor can only judge the likelihood of various outcomes based on the information available at the time of the decision. Consequently, if an outcome evaluated as a remote possibility at the statement date does happen to occur, that eventuality does not invalidate the reasonableness of the judgment.

The following case illustrates the process of evaluating the likelihood of outcome before comparing the potential dollar magnitude of an uncertainty concerning the tax liability to the normal bases of comparison in financial statements.

In 1965 the Internal Revenue Service commenced a review of prior-year returns of the client. The agent assigned worked substantially on a full-time basis from 1965 to 1971 before he disclosed to client personnel the adjustments he intended to propose. In connection with our examination of the September 30, 1971, financial statements, we reviewed the agent's informal proposals and classified the potential tax liability that would affect net assets for years under review and subsequent years that could be affected, as shown in the table opposite.

Our overall evaluation of the agent's proposals indicated a maximum probable liability upon settlement of the issues of about $200,000 for years through 1970 and about $20,000 additional for the year 1971.

Although we considered it a remote possibility that the agent's positions with respect to most of the major issues could be sustained, we also considered that the maximum potential tax liability was relatively immaterial, and accordingly we did not modify our opinion to make reference to the tax review. Our guidelines were:

---

[3] *Ibid.*, pp. 3-4.

1. *Retained earnings were $860,000. Although both the maximum probable liability ($220,000) and the maximum possible liability ($820,000) were material as related solely to the retained earnings balance, retained earnings would have little significance to an investor in the Company's stock. No dividends had ever been paid, and none could be expected in view of the Company's capital structure and announced intentions. The balance of retained earnings amounted to only 4¢ per share of stock outstanding; the market value of the Company's common stock (about $2 per share) was based on potential appreciation in land values rather than near-term dividend expectations.*

2. *Total shareholder equity was $24,400,000. Total assets were $39,500,000.*

3. *A net loss of $236,000 was incurred during the year ended 1971. Increase of the loss by even $70,000 would not affect earnings trends, nor could it be expected to affect any decisions by an investor in the Company's stock.*

Because of the significant amount of possible assessment (as opposed to the relative significance), we suggested that the client disclose in a footnote to the financial statements the income tax review

Table of Potential Tax Liability

	1965-1969 (Years Under Review)	1970	1971	Total
Excellent chance that proposed assessment cannot be sustained	$130,000	$ —	$ —	$130,000
Good chance that proposed assessment cannot be sustained	240,000	60,000	40,000	340,000
Average chance that proposed assessment cannot be sustained	26,000	—	—	26,000
Considered that issues must be compromised at substantially less than proposed amounts	110,000	170,000	30,000	310,000
Agent has good chance of sustaining assessment	14,000	—	—	14,000
	$520,000	$230,000	$70,000	$820,000

and the maximum amount of tax that might be claimed. We considered this desirable since it would permit interested parties to apply their own guidelines of materiality to the contingent liability.

Although the final decision in this case was that the exception was not material enough to require even a qualified opinion, the same sort of evaluation can be applied to any exception based on uncertainty.

In an evaluation of the uncertainty of outcome of an event, the auditor must consider the *imminence* of the event and the relevance of past *experience* as a guide to making a reasonable estimate of the outcome. The resolution of the tax agent's proposals in the case presented was imminent. On the other hand, the auditor had relevant past experience to draw upon in making the evaluation.

Conversely, if the ultimate resolution of an uncertainty is not imminent, there is a corresponding reduction in any presumption that would indicate the need for a disclaimer. Potential relative magnitude must be combined with an evaluation of probability to determine the *expected* magnitude of an event. Distance on the time horizon reduces the expected magnitude with respect to the current financial statements. In addition, the company has time to plan to absorb the impact of the event if adverse.

Utility. Once a determination has been made that the expected relative magnitude of an uncertainty-based exception is large enough to require an exception in the audit report, attention shifts to reporting utility as the primary determinant of whether a qualified opinion or disclaimer of opinion is appropriate. Dollar magnitude is of little relative importance once the auditor has decided to, at least, qualify his opinion.

Nature of Item. Consideration of the nature of the item causing the exception is an excellent example of the role of *presumption* in the reporting decision process. Certain factors create a presumption that a given type of report is appropriate. That presumption must then be examined in more detail to determine whether the general presumption should hold. For example, in the case previously presented, the potential relative magnitude of the tax liability which would result from the tax agent's examination might have created a presumption for an exception in the audit report. However, further analysis of the probability of the potential liability revealed that the expected relative magnitude was not material, and an unqualified opinion was issued.

In considering the nature of the item causing the exception, the most significant aspect of the evaluation is determination of whether the item is a general condition or a specific, localized matter. An exception which indicates a general condition is not an appropriate subject for qualification and creates the presumption that a disclaimer of opinion should be issued. Unless the general condition can be reduced to a more localized and specific problem, the auditor should disclaim an opinion.

The most common example of an uncertainty-based general condition is doubt about whether the company is a going concern. Going-concern problems are significant enough to require special attention, and the next chapter explores the subject, including the decision process of reducing a general condition to a specific exception.

Specific, localized uncertainties are not infrequent; contingent liabilities and the doubtful recovery of assets are common examples. In these cases, there is a presumption, if the item is material, that a qualified opinion should be issued. While a further detailed analysis of the exception-causing item may indicate that no qualification is necessary, or in some unusual cases that a disclaimer is appropriate, a qualified opinion would be expected as a general rule.

Expertise. Financial statement users have certain reasonable expectations about the type of responsibility assumed by the auditor in the expression of an opinion on the statements. The reporting criterion of expertise as it relates to exceptions based on uncertainty concerns the appropriateness of the auditor shifting responsibility for certain evaluations to the reader of his report. Accordingly, as a reporting concept, expertise has a bearing on questions such as the appropriate use of the "subject to" or the "except for" forms of qualified opinion, and the distinction between an adverse opinion and a disclaimer of opinion in the case of pervasive exceptions.

When an auditor issues an unqualified opinion, the reasonable expectation of report readers is that he has satisfied himself as to the fair presentation of the statements in conformity with generally accepted accounting principles by performing any auditing procedures and by making any required judgments which within his professional competence as an auditor are necessary to forming an opinion.

Conversely, when an auditor issues a qualified opinion or a disclaimer of opinion because of an uncertainty, the reasonable expectation of a reader of the report should be that the auditor was not able to evaluate the impact of the exception on the financial statements. In other words, the matter should not be within the expertise of the auditor. No audit procedures should exist which the auditor could feasibly apply to obtain satisfaction.

Normally, uncertainties relating to the realization of assets are resolved by economic events subsequent to the date of financial statements. This is particularly true of current assets, such as marketable securities. Ordinarily the auditor should be able to form a judgment on the realizability of such assets; they are not appropriate subject matter for a "subject to" opinion. This does not mean that the auditor will always be able to express an unqualified opinion on such assets. If the auditor believes management's judgment as to realizability is incorrect, an "except for" qualification may be appropriate. On the other hand, unusual circumstances may take the evaluation of the realizability of an asset outside the area of competence of an auditor. For example, evaluation of the realizability of marketable securities, though subject to uncertainty, is normally within the auditor's competence. However, some securities do not have a ready market value, and evaluation of their realizability requires subjective judgments which may not be within the auditor's competence.

Open-ended investment companies must reflect all assets at current value, showing cost parenthetically. If an investment company's portfolio of securities contains investments for which market quotations are not readily available, the board of directors must determine the "fair value" of the securities. The uncertainties inherent in the determination of fair value for these securities place them beyond the auditor's competence to evaluate. This problem was recognized in a pertinent release of the SEC.

In December 1970, the Securities and Exchange Commission issued Accounting Series Release No. 118, titled "Accounting for Investment Securities by Registered Investment Companies." The release, which supplements ASR No. 113 on the evaluation of "restricted" securities, deals with securities valued in good faith by the directors of an investment company. ASR No. 118 provides that in some cases the auditors of investment companies may issue qualified opinions with "subject to" exceptions. The following passage from ASR No. 118 indicates the SEC's recognition that evaluation of the realizability of this type of asset is not within the auditor's competence:

> In the case of securities carried at "fair value" as determined by the Board of Directors in "good faith," the accountant does not function as an appraiser and is not expected to substitute his judgment for that of the company's directors; rather, he should review all information considered by the board or by analysts reporting to it, read relevant minutes of directors' meetings, and ascertain the procedures followed by the directors. If the accountant is unable to express an unqualified opinion because of the uncertainty inherent in the valuations of the securities based on the directors' subjective judgment, he should nevertheless make appropriate mention in his certificate whether in the circumstances the procedures appear to be reasonable and the underlying documentation appropriate.

In these circumstances, ASR No. 118 recommends suitable language for expressing a qualified opinion as follows:

> As discussed more fully [in] Note 1 to the financial statements, securities amounting to $_____ (____% of net assets) have been valued at fair value as determined by the Board of Directors. We have reviewed the procedures applied by the directors in valuing such securities and have inspected underlying documentation; while in the circumstances the procedures appear to be reasonable and the documentation appropriate, determination of fair values involves subjective judgment which is not susceptible to substantiation by auditing procedures.
>
> In our opinion, subject to the effect on the financial statements of the valuation of securities determined by the Board of Directors as described in the preceding paragraph, the (financial statements) present fairly. . . .

The auditor must still apply all feasible auditing procedures and make those evaluations which are within his competence. If the auditor's examination discloses that the directors' valuation procedures are inadequate or unreasonable, or if the underlying documentation does not appear to support the valuation, then he must qualify his opinion with an "except for" introduction with respect to the securities carried at "fair value." The exception should relate to lack of conformity with generally accepted accounting principles. In this case, the security valuation procedures prescribed by the SEC for investment companies constitute the necessary substantial authoritative support. Perhaps a useful rule of thumb for taking exception would be that when the auditor cannot make the positive representations found in the explanatory middle paragraph of the recommended "subject to" opinion, then an "except for" opinion is appropriate for all or a significant portion of the securities being valued.

For some uncertainties outside the auditor's competence to evaluate, the opinion of an expert may be used. Frequently, the role of other experts is to place limits on the financial statement impact of the uncertainty so that the auditor may evaluate its relative magnitude.

For example, the following case illustrates the use of the opinion of an attorney on a major liability.

During 1970 two lawsuits were filed against the client and several other defendants asserting claims based upon the conduct of the business by the previous management. The client has been advised by legal counsel that it is not possible to forecast the outcome of this litigation or the ultimate effect on financial condition because of many unsettled legal issues and uncertainties about the facts. However, the client has also been advised by counsel that its cross claim against its former independent public accountants has merit and that if they should be held liable in this litigation, they should prevail in a cross claim for the amount of the liability.

The financial statements did not establish parameters on liability if the client were held liable in this litigation, so initially our thinking was to consider the effect assuming complete loss of shareholders' equity. We considered such loss to be material to the financial statements taken as a whole.

Subsequently, we learned that the client's attorneys had made a computation of the maximum liability in the event of adverse decisions in all the litigation. We obtained a letter of opinion from the attorneys stating such maximum liability at $4,000,000. In addition, we secured a copy of the attorneys' opinion that if the client were held liable in this litigation, its cross claim should prevail.

We concluded that the maximum liability in the event of adverse decisions in all the litigation did not have a material effect on the financial statements.

The financial position of the client may be summarized as follows:

12/31/70

Current assets	$ 70,000,000
Other assets	18,000,000
Plant and equipment, net	20,000,000
Total assets	$108,000,000
Current liabilities	(28,000,000)
Shareholders' equity	$ 80,000,000

The attorney's letter addressed to the president read as follows:

"You have asked our opinion as to what the maximum possible liability of your Company would be if it is unsuccessful in its defense of the X and Y cases.

"It is our opinion that the maximum possible liability of the Company in the X case would be in the neighborhood of $2,000,000. The class of stockholders on whose behalf the plaintiff is suing does not include W corporation. It is our opinion that the maximum possible liability of the Company in the Y case would be in the neighborhood of $3,500,000 to $4,000,000. The class of stockholders on whose behalf the plaintiff in the Y case is suing does include W Corporation. The two cases are class actions and therefore (except for W Corporation in the Y case and other possible minor discrepancies between the classes involved in the two cases) a judgment for the plaintiff in either one of them would preclude a judgment in the other. As a consequence, the possible maximum liabilities in the two cases should not be cumulative.

"We have not discounted the maximum liabilities to which the Company is exposed in these two cases by our opinion as to the merits of the Company's defenses or by our evaluation of any other strategic considerations favorable to the Company in these litigations. And we have not taken into account any possible federal income tax benefit to the Company which might result from the payment of any judgment.

"There are also possible legal theories which if they were accepted by the courts might support setting the amounts of the possible liabilities of the Company in these cases at higher figures. However, the court decisions so far have shown little inclination to accept these theories, and we believe that it is unlikely that they would be accepted in this case."

In the financial statements, the liability was disclosed in the following footnote:

"During 1970, two lawsuits were filed against the Company and several other defendants asserting claims based upon the conduct of the business by the previous management. The Company has been informed by legal counsel that it is not possible to forecast the outcome of this litigation or its ultimate effect on the Company's financial condition because it involves many unsettled legal issues and uncertainties about the facts. However, the Company has been advised by its legal counsel that the Company's cross claim against its former independent public accountants, who also are defendants in these lawsuits, has substantial merit and that if the Company should be held liable in these lawsuits it should prevail in its cross claim for the amount of its liability.

"Following an investigation, early in 1970, by independent legal counsel of the conduct of the Company's business by the previous management, the Company filed suit for damages against three former officers and the estate of the deceased former chairman and president. The ultimate effect of this lawsuit upon the Company's financial condition cannot be evaluated at this time."

This discussion is not intended to be definitive on the use of other experts, but when the auditor relies on the opinion of another expert for matters wholly outside his competence, ordinarily he need not go behind the representations of the other expert. His responsibility is ordinarily discharged as long as his reliance is reasonable.

Pervasiveness. In evaluating reporting utility, one of the key determinations made by the auditor concerns pervasiveness of an uncertainty-based exception. If an exception can be isolated and the significance of the exception for the financial statements is apparent, a qualified opinion adequately communicates the situation to the report reader. On the other hand, if the exception permeates the financial statements to such an extent that appraisal of the statements is virtually impossible, a qualified opinion is not justified.

Pervasive uncertainties are basically of two types: (1) uncertainties that imperil the continued existence of an entity and (2) uncertainties that have a strong degree of relationship to entity operations and that are interrelated to a number of financial statement items. In practice, the most common cause of a disclaimer of opinion is an uncertainty that constitutes a peril to the continued existence of the entity.

Although the existence of uncertainties of a rather large relative magnitude are not uncommon, they do not very frequently lead to a disclaimer of opinion. Many uncertainties, such as contingent liabilities or questionable recovery of assets, place a strain on a company's finances but do not imperil its continued existence. In most instances, these uncertainties, though of large magnitude, can be isolated, and their impact on the financial statements can be adequately described in a qualified opinion. Since no audit procedures could feasibly be applied to allow the auditor to form a judgment on the uncertainty, the burden of evaluation should be shifted to the report reader.

Uncertainties that imperil the continued existence of an entity will usually be evaluated as a general condition under the reporting criterion of "nature of item." The next chapter considers that type of uncertainty. However, an isolable matter may be so important that continued existence is seriously imperiled and a disclaimer of opinion is necessary, as the following case indicates.

In mid-1965, Citisan, Inc., completed construction of a refuse disposal facility on land leased from the city. The facility has been operated since then (with some technical difficulties) under a refuse disposal contract with the city.

Our report on the consolidated financial statements for the year ended September 30, 1967, was dated November 22, 1967, and contained a "subject to recovery of investment in plant" qualification.

In December, 1967, a citizen's committee was activated, with the approval of the company, as a result of complaints from citizens of the community during 1966 and 1967 that the plant generated odors and was a public nuisance. Upon receiving the report of the special committee, the city council terminated the refuse disposal contract on February 6, 1968.

The contract cancellation and resulting suspension of operations were of such significance that we revised our next report from a "subject to" to a "no overall" opinion.

Although questionable recovery of the investment in the plant was an isolable uncertainty adequately described by a qualified opinion, cancellation of the contract to operate the plant jeopardized the continued existence of the entity—since its sole activity was operation of the plant—and made a qualified opinion inappropriate.

An isolable uncertainty which nevertheless has a pervasive impact on the financial statements may also relate to a liability. The following case illustrates an uncertainty surrounding a potential liability that was significant enough to imperil the continued existence of the entity.

EIE Warehousing, Inc. stored goods for various customers and controlled these goods by use of perpetual inventory records on tab card equipment. The perpetual records were the source of monthly statements to customers and the basis of billings for storage.

Our audit work included a test of the perpetual records by comparing reported balances to a physical count of inventory actually on hand and by circularization of reported balances with customers. Both procedure tests disclosed differences over and under which could not be satisfactorily reconciled. None of the differences was significant, but almost all test counts had differences.

The significance of the errors in the company's records could not be easily determined. Our tests covered only a minor portion of the total inventory quantity on hand. The estimated value of the stored goods was between $25 and $35 million. Based upon the company's financial position, a 1% ($250,000) error would be significant.

The financial position at July 31, 1969, date of the audit, was:

Assets	*$325,000*
Liabilities	*475,000*
Shareholders' equity (deficit)	*(150,000)*
	$325,000

We felt that due to the significance of the potential liability compared to the company's financial position, we could not render an opinion on the company's financial statements as a whole. The fact that differences were in no particular direction (over and under) served to support our feeling regarding the lack of control over stored goods. Our report included the following:

The realization of equipment and improvements ($190,000) is dependent upon the success of future operations together with the ability to maintain financing arrangements.

Our tests of the Company's control over stored goods disclosed over and under differences between recorded and actual quantities on hand and those quantities confirmed in writing by customers. As a result of our tests and the significance of the Company's responsibility for such goods, the potential liability cannot be determined at July 31, 1969.

Because of the significance of the matters referred to in the preceding paragraphs, we are unable to express an opinion on the accompanying financial statements taken as a whole.

The other type of pervasive uncertainty—one which materially affects a significant number of financial statement items—is possible but not probable under present reporting criteria. No examples based on this type of uncertainty were disclosed. Conceivably, if a major portion of revenue is subject to uncertainty, such as in renegotiation cases, the impact on the income statement may be so extensive that no meaningful opinion can be expressed. However, a large enough portion of revenue is not usually subject to uncertainty to preclude an opinion.

Carman Blough describes a problem submitted to the Institute's technical information service in which all of a company's sales were made to a single corporate customer controlled by the same person, who was chief executive officer of the client company. Since the sales were not made at arm's-length, Mr. Blough believed that the auditor should disclaim an opinion. He reasoned as follows:

> It seems to us that the condition of the business and the results of its operations are so dependent upon the whim of the owner that they could be changed momentarily without any change in business conditions. Furthermore, they do not necessarily represent the earning capacity of the business in a competitive market. There has been no arms-length bargaining in the fixing of the selling price, which might be substantially more or substantially less if it had been determined in the open market. Conceivably, of course, the prices might be the same as would have resulted from arms-length bargaining but no reliance can be placed on that possibility.
>
> A major purpose of financial statements is to be of use in reaching conclusions as to the probable future of a business. It is difficult to see how the financial statements of the client company could, in themselves, serve that purpose. Undoubtedly, as an historical document they would be of value to the management and have some use to others but certainly the prospective creditor or investor would find them unreliable guides in judging the future.
>
> Accordingly, in our opinion, the auditor in such a case should deny an opinion as to the over-all fairness of the statements and clearly state his reasons for doing so.[4]

This case also emphasizes the importance of the directing concept of utility in the reporting decision. However, the case is an isolated

---

[4]Carman G. Blough, "Sales Not at Arms-length," *The Journal of Accountancy*, September 1960, p. 73.

example, and despite the *possibility* of the second type of pervasive uncertainty, the fact remains that it is extremely rare. The predominant type of uncertainty sufficient to require a disclaimer of opinion is the pervasive uncertainty which indicates that the continued existence of an entity is imperiled.

Comprehensive Consideration of Reporting Concepts

Not all the directing concepts are relevant to every reporting decision; and even when a specific type of exception is considered, such as an unusual uncertainty, not every aspect of every concept need apply. However, the following case is presented as a convenient vehicle for a comprehensive review of many relevant reporting concepts. The case is largely confined to a statement of the facts and the reporting decision made, with an explication of the decision following.

The client operates travel tours, primarily in the continental United States. In October 1969, the company contracted with a charter airline for air transportation for a series of fifty all-inclusive tours to be conducted during 1970. Payments by the company for this transportation were to total $1,650,000. This was a fixed cost and only minor reductions were provided in the event of cancellation of a flight. The company's condensed balance sheet at December 31, 1969 (audit date) was as follows:

Current assets	*$400,000*
Receivables from officers and affiliated companies	*125,000*
Cash value of life insurance	*90,000*
Equipment and improvements	*60,000*
	$675,000
Current liabilities	*600,000*
Common stock	*15,000*
Retained earnings	*60,000*
	$675,000

The company showed a small net income in 1969, after substantial losses in 1967 and 1968.

The president of the company was optimistic about the success of the program because of the good market potential and the attractive selling price of the tours. The controller was somewhat less optimistic because of the large increase in sales (about 30 per cent necessary and a high break-even point of about 80 per cent of capacity). Neither the company nor the industry had had any previous experience with this type of tour program.

We had no basis for a conclusion that the program would not be successful, but the high requirements for its success made substantial losses a distinct possibility. It was also clear that payment of the obligation was tied to the success of tour sales.

Because of these uncertainties and the materiality of the item, we decided to qualify our report as follows:

As explained in Note 1 to the accompanying financial statements, as of December 31, 1969, the Company had contracted for chartered air transportation, totaling $1,650,000, to be provided in connection with a new 1970 tour program. The Company's ability to meet this obligation is dependent upon the future success of the program.

In our opinion, subject to the effect of the outcome of the matter described in the preceding paragraph, the accompanying financial statements. . . .

The commitment was shown on the balance sheet as a memorandum amount:

Commitment for Future Tours (Note 1)   *$1,650,000*

Note 1 read as follows:

As of December 31, 1969, the Company had contracted for chartered air transportation to be provided for fifty tours to be conducted in 1970. The contract provides for total payments by the Company of $1,650,000, irrespective of the volume of sales applicable to these tours.

The concept of selling tours under chartered arrangements is new to the Company. The success of this program will depend upon the net revenues to be received. The Company is of the opinion that the program will be successfully operated, and accordingly, no provision has been made in the accounts as of December 31, 1969, for possible loss under the contract.

The success of the company's undertaking was definitely uncertain, and the relative magnitude of its commitment at over twenty times the net assets of the company was material even though limits were not placed on the potential loss. Thus, an exception based on uncertainty existed. While management believed the program would be successful, the link to past experience was nonexistent, and the uncertainty was unusual.

In evaluating the probability of the uncertainty, consideration of "experience" was more difficult than consideration of "imminence." The matter would be resolved within the next year. Relating the reasonableness of management's judgment about the future to past experience was not possible since the company had no experience with the type of program under consideration. In addition, analogous past experience could not be considered since the type of program involved was new to the industry. Without *any* experience, a possibility existed that no qualification was appropriate since no evidence existed for a judgment. However, the high break-even point and the related large increase in sales required raised the possibility of a substantial imminent loss. Nevertheless, there was no basis for a judgment that a loss had been incurred.

The final reporting decision was that greatest utility was achieved by a qualified opinion. The uncertainty could be isolated for the attention of the report reader so that the burden of evaluation could be placed on the report reader. The auditor had available no special expertise which better equipped him to make the evaluation. As long as the report called the reader's attention to the uncertainty, the reader benefited in knowing that in other respects the financial statements conformed to accepted standards.

Addendum—A Reporting Dilemma

Before leaving the subject of exceptions based on uncertainty, a related subject deserves attention. This chapter has dealt with the criteria for deciding when a disclaimer of opinion is more appropriate than a qualified opinion. However, the directing reporting concepts provide little definitive guidance on a related question. When is the "subject to" form of qualification more appropriate than the "except for" form and, a more basic question, is the distinction between the two meaningful?

A survey of the literature on reporting (Chapter 2) indicates that prior to 1962 the two forms of qualification were used interchangeably. SAP No. 32 restricted the "subject to" form to qualifications based on unusual uncertainties. An SEC release of concurrent vintage, ASR No. 90, indicated that qualifications based on such uncertainties were acceptable in filings with the Commission, and the phrase "subject to " became the flag under which qualifications could pass through the SEC. However, the relation between "subject to" and unusual uncertainties is an artificiality created by SAP No. 32, and the SEC release designated only the subject matter of an acceptable qualification and not an acceptable phrase.

The directing reporting concepts shed little light on the question. As an aspect of the utility concept, the "expertise" criterion indicates that if a matter is within his competence the auditor should evaluate it and come to a definite reporting conclusion. For example, the auditor should form a definite judgment on the adequacy of the allowance for uncollectible accounts. If he believes it inadequate, he should propose an adjustment of the allowance and, if the client rejects the adjustment, an "except for" qualification is appropriate rather than the "subject to" form. Estimation of uncollectible accounts is an approximation inherent in the accounting process and, as such, is within the auditor's competence. However, the probability of collection of an extremely material receivable may rest on an unusual uncertainty, such as a disputed contract, which is not within the competence of the auditor to evaluate. The key is not the asset classification but the relevance of the auditor's expertise. Thus, the use of the "subject to" form has potential for abuse since it may be used when the auditor could form a judgment but declines that judgment. The appropriateness of the *form* of qualification cannot be evaluated by reference to externally observable criteria, such as asset classification. Although the "subject to" qualification calls the report reader's attention to the matter, report utility may not be achieved because an evaluation the auditor is competent to make may have been shifted to the reader. The directing concept crystallizes the problem, but does not contribute to its solution.

Guiding concepts hold some potential for a solution, but they are in the nature of goals and not really suitable for definitive solution of a reporting problem. One of the guiding concepts—environment—lends significance to the "subject to" versus "except for" question. An awareness of the regulatory environment indicates that the SEC may accept a "subject to" qualification, while an "except for" qualification would call for *correction* of the financial statements.

Consideration of the guiding concept of "communication" raises the question of whether the distinction between the two forms of qualification has any significance to the average report reader. While the question is researchable, an *a priori* analysis seems sufficient. The full impact of the distinction cannot be known to a report reader unless he has read AICPA pronouncements on reporting. While Accounting Principles Board Opinions have received a fair amount of attention from nonaccountants, few nonaccountants are probably aware of the existence of the Committee on Auditing Procedure. Few average readers probably have any facility in distinguishing the niceties of expression used in modification of the standard short-form report.

Perhaps in recognition of the problem, the SEC "protects" the average report reader by requiring correction of statements on which an "except for" qualification is expressed, while accepting "subject to" qualifications. However, in some cases this administrative policy only aggravates the problem. The research for this monograph disclosed isolated incidents in which reports accepted by the SEC contained two qualifications—one an uncertainty, the other a departure from generally accepted accounting principles. Invariably the uncertainty matter was placed first in the qualification with a "subject to" introductory phrase, while the accounting departure followed without an "except for" introduction and with an explanation that in some cases did not mention generally accepted accounting principles. Under the banner of "subject to," the qualification was accepted.

Reporting criteria cannot provide a definitive solution. No matter how clear the criteria, noncompliance is always possible. However, the present vagueness of existing criteria has probably contributed to the problem, and the policy of the SEC has heightened the importance of the matter.

Three alternative solutions are worthy of consideration.

1. *Abandonment of the Distinction.* The distinction between the "except for" form of qualification and the "subject to" form could be abandoned altogether. All qualifications would be introduced by the same introductory phrase—either "except for" or some other suitably strong language of exception. The qualification—no matter what its cause—is an indication that with the exception of the matter causing qualification the financial statements are fairly presented. The audit report would also have to specify the cause of the exception so as to indicate which of the three following possible causes of exception existed:

a. The auditor was unable to form a judgment on a designated financial statement item because he did not apply feasible auditing procedures and does not know what adjustments of the statements might be required if the procedures were applied.

b. The auditor believes that a specific financial statement item is not fairly presented and believes that adjustment of the statements would result in a fair presentation.

c. An uncertainty exists which precludes both the auditor and the client from knowing what adjustment of the statements, if any, would result in a fair presentation.

2. *Refinement of the Distinction.* New and more definitive guidelines for use of the "subject to" form of qualification could be instituted. The choice between the two forms of qualification could be related to more observable matters so that departures from reporting guidelines are more apparent. For example, the form of qualification could be related to the prior period adjustment criteria of APB Opinion

No. 9 on reporting the results of operations. In addition, when both an uncertainty and a departure from generally accepted accounting principles exist, reporting guidelines could specify that the "except for" qualification takes precedence and should come first rather than being buried behind a "subject to" qualification.

3. *Retention With Communication.* Present guidelines could be retained and coupled with an educational campaign directed at report readers to explain the meaning of various report qualifications.

Choosing among these alternatives requires value judgments which have no particular significance when made by an individual observer. There are many considerations. Adoption of the first alternative would increase the SEC's administrative burden since the introductory phrase of the qualification would no longer signal its acceptability. The effectiveness of an educational campaign would depend largely on the quality of its execution and the receptiveness and capabilities of report readers. In the final analysis, any change would have *some* merit since the attention of auditors would be called to the matter, and their increased level of consciousness about the problem should result in improved reporting.

6

Pervasive Uncertainties—
Going-Concern Problems

Uncertainties that imperil the continued existence of an entity may be characterized as going-concern reporting problems. Uncertainties of this type are by definition pervasive, and this chapter presents a detailed explanation of the pervasiveness criterion applied to going-concern problems.

The Nature and Significance
of the Going-Concern Concept

The idea of a "going concern" is basic to accounting theory. There is substantial agreement on its meaning and role in financial statement preparation.

Position in Accounting Theory. APB Statement No. 4 recognizes the going-concern concept as a "basic feature" of financial accounting determined by the characteristics of the financial accounting environment and describes it as follows:

> *Going concern* —continuation of entity operations is usually assumed in financial accounting in the absence of evidence to the contrary.[1]

Statement No. 4 indicates that the complex task of measuring economic activity is given underlying continuity and stability by the

---

[1]"Basic Concepts and Accounting Principles Underlying Financial Statements of Business Enterprises," Statement of the Accounting Principles Board 4, AICPA, New York, October 1970, p. 10.

following elements of modern economic organization:

(1) Several forms of enterprise, especially the corporate form, continue to exist as legal entities for extended periods of time.

(2) The framework of law, custom, and traditional patterns of action provides a significant degree of stability to many aspects of the economic environment. In a society in which property rights are protected, contracts fulfilled, debts paid, and credit banking and transfer operations efficiently performed, the degree of uncertainty is reduced and the predictability of the outcome of many types of economic activities is correspondingly increased.[2]

Apparently, Statement No. 4 presents these factors as justifying the use of the going-concern concept as a device for resolution of uncertainty in accounting measurement. Uncertainty is avoided by assuming that the entity being accounted for has an indefinite life until some major event indicates contrary evidence.

Several other notable contributions to accounting literature have advanced the concept of a going concern. Accounting Research Study No. 1, *The Basic Postulates of Accounting*, by Moonitz, and Accounting Research Study No. 7, *Inventory of Generally Accepted Accounting Principles for Business Enterprises*, by Grady, both contain similar expressions of the concept. Grady explains it as follows:

. . .a large part of accounting practice as well as theory is based on the presumption that the accounting entity will continue in operation and not be liquidated in the foreseeable future. In the absence of evidence to the contrary, the entity should be viewed as remaining in operation indefinitely. . . .Indefinite continuance means that the business will not be liquidated within a span of time necessary to carry out present contractual commitments or to use up assets according to the plans and expectations presently held. This view makes the concept a tentative judgment, subject to revision in the future as contractual agreements are changed and plans and expectations with respect to operations shift.[3]

An earlier publication by the American Accounting Association included "enterprise continuity" as an underlying concept and commented as follows:

The "going-concern" concept assumes the continuance of the general enterprise situation. In the absence of evidence to the contrary, the entity is viewed as remaining in operation indefinitely. Although it is recognized that business activities and economic conditions are changing constantly, the concept assumes that controlling environmental circumstances

---

[2]*Ibid.*, pp. 22-23.
[3]Paul Grady, *Inventory of Generally Accepted Accounting Principles for Business Enterprises*, Accounting Research Study No. 7, AICPA, New York, 1965, pp. 27-28.

will persist sufficiently far into the future to permit existing plans and programs to be carried to completion. Thus the assets of the enterprise are expected to have continuing usefulness for the general purpose for which they were acquired, and its liabilities are expected to be paid at maturity.

To the extent that termination of important activities can be predicted with assurance, a partial or complete abandonment of the assumption of continuity is in order. Otherwise, the assumption provides a reasonable basis for presenting enterprise status and performance.[4]

While accounting literature differs on the appropriate term to describe the going-concern idea—postulate, concept, assumption, etc.— there is substantial agreement on the meaning of the term. In accordance with the going-concern concept, an entity is presumed to continue in existence indefinitely, although not necessarily in perpetuity; however, contrary evidence may negate this assumption.

Role in Financial Statement Preparation. An important consequence of the going-concern concept in financial statement preparation is that assets include expenditures of prior years that may have little, if any, separate realizable value. An organizational or promotional expenditure in one year normally does not result in any legal property right, yet if the expenditure was made with the expectation of benefiting future operations, it is not charged off in the year of expenditure. In a similar fashion, debt discount and expense, research and development costs, and other unexpired costs with little or no separate exchange value are treated as assets on the balance sheet.

Labor and other production costs, along with allocable portions of depreciation and overhead, are aggregated with material costs to determine the value of work in process in the expectation that products will be finished and sold. These expenditures are treated as assets even though the immediate realizable value of work in process may be lower than the cost of materials before production began.

Similarly, balance sheet liabilities include certain obligations, such as amounts accrued under pension plans, that are accounted for in terms of the entity's long-range commitment rather than in the legal sense of enforceable creditor claims.

In general, unless there is an indication that termination of operations is imminent, forced-sale or liquidation values and liquidation commitments are irrelevant in financial statement preparation.

The going-concern concept also influences financial statement disclosures. Financial statement users base their decisions on the expectation of continuity of entity operations. Though external

---

[4]*Accounting and Reporting Standards for Corporate Financial Statements,* American Accounting Association, 1957, p. 2.

economic events may seriously affect operations, there is an expectation that in the absence of contrary disclosures these changes can be borne by the entity without forcing it into liquidation.

Audit Importance. The going-concern concept encompasses both the evidence-gathering and reporting aspects of the auditor's examination, but his initial consideration must be with the concept as it relates to the accumulation of audit evidence. In their development of the theory of auditing, Mautz and Sharaf incorporated the going-concern concept as an *auditing* postulate, stated as follows:

> In the absence of clear evidence to the contrary, what has held true in the past for the enterprise under examination will hold true in the future.[5]

Mautz and Sharaf felt that continuity was a necessary assumption which if released would make auditing "improbable, if not impossible."[6] They recognized that the going-concern concept of accounting was encompassed by the auditing postulate, but believed that the postulate added something more, as the following passage indicates:

> Acceptance of this postulate places important limits on the extent of an auditor's responsibilities and provides a basis for reducing the extent of his obligation to forecast the future and to have his work judged on the basis of hindsight.[7]

Thus, an unqualified opinion is in no sense a guarantee that the entity reported upon will not be liquidated in the foreseeable future or that operations will be profitable. Neither long-term nor short-term survival is warranted. An unqualified opinion means that either no evidence has come to the auditor's attention to contradict the going-concern concept, or that the auditor has evaluated known contrary evidence and concluded that it does not indicate that liquidation is imminent.

If an entity has reached the operating stage, the auditor is entitled to assume that future operations will continue unless contrary evidence comes to his attention. In the course of his examination the auditor does not actively seek to validate the going-concern status of the entity, but remains aware of the possibility that the entity is not a going concern. His experience with, or knowledge of, entities that have liquidated and his training in accounting theory—in which the going-concern concept is well recognized—make him alert to the potential

---

[5]R. K. Mautz and Hussein A. Sharaf, *The Philosophy of Auditing*, American Accounting Association, 1961, p. 42.
[6]*Ibid.*, p. 49.
[7]*Ibid.*

consequences of situations in which the entity is not a going concern. Therefore, an auditor is fully aware of the contingency of the going-concern assumption.

Naturally, the going-concern assumption is not always valid. Nevertheless, in the absence of evidence to the contrary, the auditor should assume that the entity is a going concern. If successful operations were predictable, there would be no risk in economic activity. However, the auditor does not assume that liquidation is impossible. Although he plans his examination as if the assumption were true, his mind is not closed to the possibility that in a given examination the going-concern assumption may be false. He remains alert to any indication in the present examination that liquidation may be imminent. The next section is devoted to consideration of the nature of evidence which may contradict the going-concern assumption.

Indicators of Going-Concern Negation

The assumption that an entity is a going concern is made in the absence of evidence to the contrary. However, what constitutes contrary evidence? Evidence about the going-concern status of an entity may be broadly classified into three categories.

First, the entity may have a record of profits and expanding operations. For this type of entity, no contrary evidence exists and the entity is, prima facie, a going concern. At the other extreme is the entity that is not, prima facie, a going concern. When an entity is in a state of bankruptcy or of liquidation and has completed the sale of its assets, evidence that contradicts the going-concern assumption is certainly present. In the same category are entities whose managements have voluntarily decided to limit their future lives, such as entities created for a specific purpose and terminated at the completion of that purpose. Neither of these categories creates difficult problems of evidence evaluation in judging going-concern status.

On the other hand, difficult evidence evaluation problems do exist for any entity having a combination of continued operating losses or involuntary conversions and their related problems, contingent liabilities, and major assets of doubtful recoverability—all of which imperil its continued existence. This section is devoted to an analysis of contrary evidence for entities falling within this category.

Elements of Contrary Evidence. Financial statements are used to appraise the financial condition of the issuing company and the effectiveness of its management in earning a return on its invested capital. A financially healthy company is characterized by adequate return on investment and sound financial position. When the converse of these two interrelated characteristics exists, the company may have a going-concern problem.

The elements of contrary evidence may be classified as follows:

A. Financing problems—difficulty in meeting obligations.

   1. Liquidity deficiency—the company's current liabilities exceed its current assets, which results in difficulty in meeting current obligations.

   2. Equity deficiency—the company's solvency is questionable because of a retained earnings deficit or, in more extreme cases, an excess of total liabilities over total assets.

   3. Debt default—the company has been unable to meet debt payment schedules or has violated one or more other covenants of its loan agreements.

   4. Funds shortage—the company has either limited or no ability to obtain additional funds from various capital sources.

B. Operating problems—apparent lack of operating success.

   1. Continued operating losses—no net profit has been earned for more than one past period.

   2. Prospective revenues doubtful—revenue is insufficient for day-to-day operating needs, or there have been cut-backs in operations, such as personnel reductions.

   3. Ability to operate is jeopardized—legal proceedings related to operations may severely curtail operations, or suppliers of operating materials may refuse to transact with the company.

   4. Poor control over operations—the company management has been unable to control operations, as evidenced by repetitive, uncorrected problems.

Financing and operating problems are related and interdependent. A series of operating losses creates an equity deficiency, and inadequate current and prospective revenues contribute to a liquidity deficiency. On the other hand, the two areas may be somewhat independent; a company may correct its operating problems, for example, but continue to have difficulties in obtaining financing.

Evaluation of Contrary Evidence. Although all of these elements are indicators of contrary evidence, no single factor or combination of factors is controlling in the decision to disclaim an opinion. Of all the elements, a net operating loss in the current year is the most prevalent among companies receiving a disclaimer of opinion, but even this element does not necessitate a disclaimer.

When all elements are present, an analysis of the contrary evidence will generally lead to a conclusion that liquidation is imminent. The following case illustrates the presence of most elements.

We were engaged to examine the financial statements of SIT, Inc., and its subsidiaries as of October 31, 1969; the companies manufacture one product used by a major manufacturing industry.

The consolidated liabilities exceeded the assets. The companies were producing very few units and had suffered substantial losses for several years. In addition, several creditors were taking legal action against the company, and its patent was due to expire in approximately 18 months. Due to this serious financial position, we realized that we would not be able to express any opinion on the financial statements; however, the stockholders wanted audited financial statements to have a reliable basis on which to decide what to do about the companies.

Condensed consolidated financial statements of the companies as of October 31, 1969, were as follows:

Balance Sheet—October 31, 1969

Current assets	$ 80,000
Property and equipment (net)	90,000
	$170,000
Current liabilities	$210,000
Contingencies	
Common stock	255,000
Retained earnings (deficit)	(295,000)
	$170,000

Statement of Loss and Deficit
For the Year Ended October 31, 1969

Sales	$ 80,000
Cost of sales	$(130,000)
Gross loss	$ (50,000)
Expenses	120,000
Net loss	$(170,000)
Deficit, November 1, 1968	(125,000)
Deficit, October 31, 1969	$(295,000)

After our standard scope paragraph, the second and third paragraphs of our report, dated February 11, 1970, were as follows:

The following matters, which are set forth more fully in the accompanying financial statements, indicate that the Company and its Subsidiaries are in serious financial condition:

(1) The Companies are sustaining continuing losses.

(2) The Companies' liabilities exceed their assets.

(3) Production and sales activities have been curtailed because of the lack of working capital which is needed to meet payroll obligations and to purchase raw materials.

(4) Several creditors of the Companies are taking or proposing to take legal or other actions to obtain payment from the Companies.

(5) The Companies' patent expires on June 20, 1971, and this may have an adverse effect on the Companies' operations.

Because of the significance of the aforementioned matters, we express no opinion on the accompanying financial statements of SIT, Inc., and Subsidiary Companies as of October 31, 1969.

In the case illustrated, the company faces an imminent threat to continuation as a going concern. Though not all of the elements of contrary evidence need be present to reach this conclusion, any other conclusion is doubtful when all elements are present. This case also raises an interesting issue which will be explored in a later chapter. Even though the examination would result in a disclaimer of opinion, "the stockholders wanted audited financial statements to have a reliable basis on which to decide what to do about the companies." The question of the utility of an auditor's report on a company with going-concern problems is significant for setting reporting prescriptions. A disclaimer in these circumstances has little, if any, utility. After completing his examination, the auditor should have formed several meaningful conclusions concerning the financial statements.

A few elements of contrary evidence may appear during a company's life, although they are not evaluated as indicating imminent liquidation. If the situation worsens and more adverse elements appear, the auditor may conclude that realization of certain operating assets is doubtful, without concluding that liquidation is imminent. Ultimately, as the passage of time adds experience, the auditor may conclude that the contrary evidence is compelling. The following case illustrates such a transition.

Pertinent financial data on SHD Co. is as follows (in thousands):

	December 31			
	1967	*1968*	*1969*	*1970*
Current assets	$ 170	$ 190	$ 580	$ 460
Current liabilities	530	570	1,000	1,110
Working capital deficit	$ 360	$ 380	$ 420	$ 650
Property, less reserves	$ 350	$ 500	$1,345	$1,700
Long-term debt	80	100	1,100	1,350
Net assets (deficit)	(90)	20	(175)	(200)
Net sales	$1,650	$1,590	$2,760	$2,880
Net income (loss)	15	90	(245)	(110)

Although the companies were in a working capital deficit position, we gave clean opinions through 1968 because they were showing profits. As explained below, we gave a "subject to" opinion for 1969 and changed to a "no opinion" for 1970.

1969

In May 1969, the client acquired an existing competitor's business (including machinery and equipment) for $700,000 payable over ten years. This plant was not operated efficiently and contributed $200,000 of the combined $245,000 loss for 1969. Between December 31, 1969, and the completion of our field work the client closed this plant and incurred additional indebtedness of $400,000 for purchase of a plant and $175,000 to meet current obligations.

Although management represented to us that the idle machinery and equipment could be utilized at other locations, they had no specific plans for its use or disposition. We seriously considered disclaiming an opinion because of (1) the significance of idle machinery and equipment and (2) the deterioration of financial position which raised a serious question as to ability to survive and, thus, a question on realization of the total investment in plant and equipment and other assets.

At the time our report was released, the client was continuing to borrow additional money on a long-term basis. In addition, the major "loss" operation for 1969 had been closed. Therefore, it was decided that a "subject to" opinion would be acceptable for 1969. Following the scope paragraph, our opinion was as follows:

> *During the year ended December 31, 1969, the SHD Co., incurred a net loss of $245,000. Also, as explained in Note 4, a substantial portion of the Companies' machinery and equipment*

($680,000) is idle as a result of the closing of the Shefield plant. Recovery of the investment in property, plant, and equipment is dependent upon successful future operations and utilization of the idle machinery and equipment at the Companies' other locations, or upon the realization of the book value of these assets on sale in the event of liquidation.

In our opinion, subject to the realization of the investment in property, plant, and equipment as explained in the preceding paragraph, the accompanying combined financial statements present fairly. . . .

1970

During 1970 the working capital deficit increased $230,000, and the companies had a net loss of $110,000. In addition, the machinery and equipment that had been idled early in 1970 was still idle; a second plant with a cost of $335,000 had been closed and was idle; and the client incurred additional indebtedness of $550,000 for the purchase of still another plant.

We concluded that under the circumstances we had no choice but to disclaim an opinion. After a typical scope paragraph, the report read as follows:

> *During the two years ended December 31, 1970, the Companies incurred substantial operating losses and as of December 31, 1970, the working capital deficit has increased to $650,000. Also, as explained in Note 3, property, plant, and equipment with an undepreciated cost of $785,000 is idle as a result of closing the Shefield and Oakford plants. Recovery of the total investment in property, plant, and equipment ($1,700,000) is dependent upon successful future operations and utilization of the idle property, plant, and equipment at other locations, or upon the realization of the book value of these assets on sale in the event of liquidation.*
>
> *Because of the significance of the matters discussed in the preceding paragraph, we are not in a position to express an overall opinion on the combined financial position of the Companies as of December 31, 1970, or the combined results of operations, or the sources and disposition of the funds for the year then ended.*

In the case illustrated, the company's difficulties began with financing problems—a working capital deficit. The working capital deficit continued for a period without the appearance of other contrary evidence. Eventually operating problems materialized which became increasingly more serious. This case points out the important role of *experience* as an evidential factor in forming a judgment on contrary evidence.

Operating problems, in particular, may exist which do not change significantly from one period to the next. However, with additional experience the auditor is in a better position to relate the reasonableness of his judgment about the future to past actions. Consequently, the auditor's evaluation may change to a greater extent than the factual circumstances.

Although, in the case illustrated, the company's difficulties began with financing problems, this does not mean that this type of progression predominates. A company may as easily experience increasingly severe operating problems for a period of time without concomitant financing problems. In addition, the severity of problems need not be balanced; financing problems, for example, may be far more severe than operating problems.

Evaluation of contrary evidence—in addition to recognition of the indicators of going-concern negation—involves analysis of factors which mitigate the elements of contrary evidence.

Mitigators of Going-Concern Negation

In addition to recognizing contrary evidence and evaluating its seriousness, the auditor must consider those factors which mitigate the contrary evidence. Evidence that financing or operating problems have been mitigated may remove the immediate threat to the continued existence of a company.

Financing problems may be mitigated by a waiver of default or an anticipated influx of funds. If there is sufficient competent evidential matter that the terms of indebtedness will be adjusted or if an arrangement actually deferring payment is obtained, the peril to the continued existence of the company may be removed. An anticipated influx of funds—if supported by evidential matter—may also remove the peril of liquidation. The influx may be from a variety of sources, such as demonstrated ability to continue borrowing, the obligation or desire of a related entity not to allow liquidation, or viable alternatives open to management in financing operations.

Evidence indicating successful future operations may be in the form of reliable company plans or budgets, or operational or management changes essential to a "turn-around" of operations. To a large extent the auditor's ability to evaluate operating problems will depend on the extent of his past experience with the company's operations. The auditor's ability to determine the reasonableness of management's estimates will be influenced both by the company's experience and his own evaluation of management's objectivity and knowledgeability concerning the subject of estimation.

After considering both the contrary evidence and any mitigating factors, the auditor considers the possible impact of losses on realization at forced liquidation values on financial position and results of operations. An important consideration in this evaluation is asset composition, which can have an important bearing on the company's ability to withstand forced liquidation.

The following three cases involving analysis of companies with operating and financing problems illustrate the evaluation of the main elements of mitigating evidence. In the first case, the evidence—including a consideration of asset composition—leads to a disclaimer, while in the second a qualified opinion is expressed. In the third case, the mitigating evidence offsets the contrary evidence, and an unqualified opinion is expressed.

Over the past four to five years, the companies have experienced many financial and management problems, the result of which has been (1) very inefficient and ineffective operational control and (2) an extremely tight and strained financial condition. In connection with a planned financial reorganization which contemplated bringing selected major creditors into the ownership picture through issuance of long-term convertible debentures, we were engaged to examine the companies' combining balance sheets as of March 31, 1970, and the related statement of income for the year then ended.

As previously stated, the companies had incurred substantial operating losses during the immediately preceding years which had resulted in a combined deficit balance in the earned surplus accounts.

The companies' plant and equipment (approximately one-third of total assets) is, for the most part, single purpose in nature, and is of little value to anyone other than another processor of like products. In addition, much of the physical plant is of the "home made" variety, and it is extremely questionable that, on a forced-sale basis, anything more than a relatively nominal amount could be realized. The plant and equipment is mostly on leased land in various locations throughout the East and Midwest.

Inventories (approximately one-third of total assets) consisted mainly of packaged product, empty containers, and raw materials. A great portion of this inventory was either unpaid for or pledged as collateral for outstanding debt.

The companies' trade and notes payable at the audit date were far past due, and it was also apparent that in addition to a complete turn-around in operations, it would also be necessary to refinance a substantial amount of debt in order for the companies to remain in operation. Subsequent to the audit date the major company in the group filed for an arrangement with creditors under Chapter XI of the Bankruptcy Act.

Considering the extremely precarious financial circumstances described above, we determined that we could not render an opinion as to the financial position of the companies on a going-concern basis.

In the second case, although the company is experiencing both financing and operating problems, sufficient mitigating evidence indicates that a qualified opinion may be expressed.

The combined balance sheet of W Co. at December 31, 1967, showed the following:

Current assets	$ 970,000
Current liabilities	1,180,000
	$ (210,000)
Investments	140,000
Plant and equipment	1,275,000
	$1,205,000
Deferred liabilities	(2,055,000)
	$ (850,000)
Share capital	175,000
Deficit	(1,025,000)
	$ (850,000)

The operations for the year resulted in a loss of about $275,000.

W Co. has a single operating branch. The branch was effectively purchased about two years ago and has not been profitable, although expanding operations indicate that a break-even volume had been reached in early 1968. Expansion has required substantial sums of money for new equipment, modification of the purchased equipment, etc., all of which has put a drain on the resources of the group. Negotiations have been in process for over a year to sell part of the share capital to outside interests. One negotiation was almost successful last year, but the purchaser was interested only in acquiring majority control.

We believed that the company needed additional capital to be able to continue operations. Although it would probably become profitable in 1968, it had obligations to pay off which would require funds in addition to those that could reasonably be expected from operations in 1968. If any of the proposed sales of part of the company were completed, the buyers would probably insist on the replacement of the existing vending equipment with that supplied by themselves. The result would be the forced scrapping of equipment before its economic life expired. On the other hand, if the operations continued, the company could expect to realize a profit with the costs of the existing equipment.

In the circumstances we believed we had to give a "subject to" opinion because of the likelihood of a forced liquidation of the equipment in the event of a purchase of part of the company. We believed such a purchase to be extremely likely because without it the company could hardly acquire the funds needed to pay off its debt.

We also considered denying an opinion because of the company's inability to survive. However, we decided this was not necessary because of the following circumstances:

---

1. The offer to acquire 51 per cent of the capital of the company was for an amount which was about twice the book value of the plant and equipment of the company, and which would have been sufficient to pay off the debt. This indicated that the company had considerable "goodwill" value even if the equipment would have to be replaced.

2. Creditors had given the company a letter indicating they would not consider the loan in default because of the late payment of the 1967 installments. The 1968 installments were not due until later this year, and the creditors had indicated they would not take advantage of the penalty clauses in the loan agreement if negotiations to acquire additional capital were still in progress at that time.

3. The shareholders of the company indicated that they would put enough capital into the company to meet any operating deficits to be incurred in the coming year.

The preceding case illustrates the reduction of a going-concern problem to an isolable matter—realization of plant and equipment— which can be adequately described by a qualified opinion. An important consideration was that the impact of partial liquidation could be absorbed by the company.

The mitigating evidence may sometimes completely counter contrary evidence so that an unqualified opinion may be expressed. The following case illustrates how substantial correction of operating problems allows the expression of an unqualified opinion.

We were engaged to examine the financial statements of Prince, Inc., as of December 31, 1970. Pertinent financial information for the company as of December 31, 1970, is presented on the page opposite.

Current assets	$ 450,000
Plant and equipment, net	275,000
Total assets	750,000
Current liabilities	400,000
Total liabilities	600,000
Stockholders' investment	150,000
Net sales (1970)	1,500,000
Net loss (1970)	100,000

In 1970 the company incurred a loss of $100,000. During the last five years the company has produced small annual net profits with the exception of 1969 when it operated at a break-even point.

During the audit we questioned the company's ability to survive and to realize its investment in plant and equipment for the following reasons:

1. The large net loss in 1970, together with the 1969 break-even operations.

2. The company has a large unit of equipment to produce a special product which, to this date, is not being utilized to capacity due to lack of sales volume.

3. Various members of management have exposed their differences of opinion to the other employees, which has contributed to employee morale problems including turnover.

We discussed the situation at length with the company president and expanded our subsequent review to substantiate certain of his remarks. After performing these steps we decided not to qualify our report on the 1970 statements for the following reasons:

1. Projected results for 1971 indicate the company will be profitable. Through April 20, 1971, the company was substantially at a break-even point due to lower sales volume than projected; however, costs were somewhat lower than budget, indicating management was exercising much needed increased cost control.

2. Through gifts in late 1969 and early 1971, most of the outstanding company stock is now held by the president. He is relatively young, aggressive and, in our opinion, capable of turning the company around.

3. The company has changed the pricing formula which has resulted in a larger sales volume of the company's more profitable products. In addition, a decision was made to reduce the amount of 1971 business done with the U.S. Government. In 1968, the company accepted an order from the U.S. Government which was too large for

the plant. As a result, production facilities were strained to a maximum resulting in inefficiencies and a large loss on the job.

4. Sales emphasis is being placed on the more profitable items.

5. As of December 31, 1970, stockholders' investment was not impaired.

According to recent statistics, the number of users of the product of the specific type made by this company is about doubling each year and, therefore, the volume of work should increase in 1971 over that of 1970.

If in 1971 the company produces only break-even results, we will definitely reconsider this problem due to the amount of current liabilities.

The foregoing cases deal primarily with the analysis of operating problems. A solution of financing problems may also be a critical factor in the analysis of mitigating evidence. In the following case, an anticipated influx of funds and evidence of future successful operations combine to allow the expression of an unqualified opinion.

Redi-Mix has two plants. The smaller plant has been operating profitably since being constructed; however, the larger plant has not operated successfully, and this fact, together with depressed prices, has caused the company substantial losses as follows:

Year Ended March 31	Net Income (Loss)
1967	$ 1,200,000
1968	(6,400,000)
1969	(4,300,000)

The loss for 1968, although huge, was not too discouraging, as the new plant commenced operations in the early part of the year and huge start-up costs were incurred—many resulting from errors in operating the plant during this learning period. Although we had considered qualifying our opinion on the March 31, 1968 financial statements, we had readily reached the conclusion that qualification at that point in time was not warranted.

The loss for 1969 was, however, greater than expected and very discouraging to the company. Continued operating problems, higher than anticipated shipping costs, and depressed selling prices were the primary causes. The company's projections for 1970 show the company about breaking even; however, we feel they are optimistic and that it is more probable that there will be a $1,000,000 to $2,000,000 loss in 1970.

A condensed balance sheet of the company as of March 31, 1969, is as follows (in thousands):

Current assets	$10,000
Plant and equipment, net	80,000
Other assets	3,000
	$93,000
Current liabilities	$ 5,000
Long-term debt	85,000
Capital stock	11,000
Accumulated deficit	(8,000)
	$93,000

We concluded that we could give an unqualified opinion as of March 31, 1969, for the following reasons:

1. There is no question that the company can continue to operate even if operating losses of approximately $2,000,000 are incurred. The majority stockholder is an international corporation with profitable worldwide operations. This stockholder has guaranteed that the company will maintain working capital of at least $4,000,000. It is not likely that they would risk the adverse effect on worldwide operations that could result from failure to provide substantial financial support to the company.

2. Of the long-term debt, $26,000,000 is payable to stockholders and subordinated to long-term debt payable to others. For this reason, the company's debt equity ratio is not representative of typical publicly held companies in the industry. If the debt to stockholders were considered equity and earnings adjusted for the annual interest charges thereon (approximately $1,700,000), the company's earnings picture would be considerably improved.

3. Beyond 1970, the company is forecasting ever-increasing profits reaching $4,700,000 before Federal income taxes in 1974. We are unable to evaluate these forecasts with any degree of reliability; however, even if the forecasts are missed by a substantial margin, the company would generate sufficient cash to liquidate its debt to third parties.

4. The industry has been burdened by over-capacity for several years. Currently, demand is retarded by the high cost of money and heavy defense spending. Trade and business publications indicate that, while the short-range outlook for improvement in the supply/demand equation is not good, the long-term outlook is better.

5. When it became apparent during 1969 that a substantial loss would be incurred, the president was replaced by a large stockholder, assisted by a representative of the largest stockholder. Since this happened, greater emphasis is being placed on accurate forecasts and control of capital expenditures and operating expenses. The marketing approach has been changed from concentration on volume to concentration on volume and profitability.

Mitigating evidence, however, often does not completely counter the contrary evidence. One illustration of the reduction of a going-concern problem to an isolable uncertainty has already been given; however, this important decision process deserves further consideration. The following case describes how evidence of a waiver of debt can reduce a going-concern problem to an isolable qualification concerning realization of assets.

One of our principal concerns at the time we issued our report was the ability of the company to obtain a further deferment of payments on a substantial amount of past due trade accounts payable. Even though we had occasion to meet with a creditors' committee, it was still a "touch and go" situation, and we had no positive assurance that the company would be successful in its attempt to secure the deferment desired. This situation, coupled with the bad operating results in 1966, clearly indicated that a disclaimer was in order. In 1967, however, the company was successful in obtaining the deferment of payables over a three-year period, and it did operate at a profit.

We decided a "subject to" on property was proper because this company did turn the corner in 1967; it was only a question of management's ability to obtain adequate interim financing and to concentrate on operations instead of selling the company.

An arrangement with creditors is not the only means of ameliorating an immediate threat to continued existence caused by financing difficulties. Although a company may be in serious financial difficulty, the alternatives open to management in the future may mitigate the impact of possible losses on financial position so that a disclaimer of opinion may not be necessary. An example follows.

The losses sustained, together with the loss of control over purchasing, have placed the company in a serious cash position. It is in default on certain of its loans and is not able to pay its bills on even a reasonably current basis. Additional financing guaranteed by a major stockholder subsequent to the year end has not alleviated this problem. The lenders have demanded that the company pledge all or substantially all of its assets. The company stated in its proxy material for its annual meeting that "in the event that the shareholders do not approve the resolutions authorizing the encumbrance of all or substantially all of the Corporation's assets, the Corporation does not know what may or can be done to obtain additional funds and to satisfy the request of the present lenders for additional security."

In addition to the significant losses and deteriorating financial condition, the company had received a number of proposals for the sale or merger of nearly all its divisions and subsidiaries. Proposals for the sale or merger of the company and its subsidiaries were being considered by the board of directors right up to our report date.

Because of the significant losses for the past two years and the other serious problems discussed above, it was necessary to review the balance sheet for realization in the event of liquidation whether by voluntary or involuntary bankruptcy or by sale or merger to a third party. We reviewed these alternatives with management in order to decide how significant the realization losses might be under those conditions.

The company might be forced into bankruptcy since the vendors and lending institutions had lost confidence in the present management. We reviewed the balance sheet with management and determined that the potential loss (including the loss from operations) in the event of bankruptcy might be as much as $4,500,000, or 50 per cent of the stockholders' investment at February 28, 1965.

Management could sell or merge parts or all of the company with one or more interested parties. Based upon our review of the proposals of three companies, the estimated realization loss on liquidation could be more than 10 per cent, but probably would be less than 50 per cent of the stockholders' investment.

Thus, if the only alternative for the company was bankruptcy, we probably would have issued a disclaimer ("no opinion" report) because of the magnitude of the uncertainties that would result. However, the management was actively pursuing with at least three companies the sale or merger route which could result in significantly less loss to the stockholders, and it was our feeling that management could avoid bankruptcy. We concluded that a "subject to" opinion was the most appropriate under the circumstances.

Since the company had a viable alternative to liquidation, the auditor was able to reduce the pervasive exception of potential liquidation to a specific qualification.

When evaluating mitigating factors, the auditor considers whether sufficient evidence exists to overcome the contrary evidence of imminent liquidation. A satisfactory arrangement with creditors or a reasonable expectation of an influx of funds may substantially correct financing difficulties. Operating problems may be substantially corrected by reasonable expectations of future successful operations.

Summary of Going-Concern Evaluation

The auditor plans his examination as if the going-concern assumption were valid for the company under examination. If in the course of his examination evidence comes to his attention which is contrary to the assumption, the auditor considers the possibility of an imminent liquidation and the impact that possible losses caused by forced liquidation would have on financial position and results of operations.

Contrary evidence normally takes the form of financing problems—such as a liquidity deficiency, an equity deficiency, debt default, and shortage of funds—or operating problems—such as continued operating losses, doubtful prospective revenues, factors jeopardizing ability to operate, and ineffective operational control. A company may experience financing or operating problems, but the consequence of these problems may be mitigated by evidence of future operating success or satisfactory resolution of financing needs. When sufficient mitigating evidence exists, the auditor may express an unqualified opinion.

If uncertainty surrounds the company's ability to absorb future operating losses and its ability to continue major projects, and if the company's ability to obtain satisfactory financing arrangements is in doubt so that continuation of the company as a going concern depends on satisfactory resolution of these matters, the auditor cannot express an unqualified or qualified opinion on the fair presentation of financial position and results of operations in conformity with generally accepted accounting principles. On the other hand, the auditor may be able to reduce the contrary evidence to an isolable uncertainty—such as uncertainty concerning the realization of inventory because of the uncertainty inherent in projected sales and costs. In this case, although a number of elements of contrary evidence may have come to the auditor's attention, he is able to conclude that there is not a substantial, imminent possibility of liquidation.

In other words, even in the face of some contrary evidence, the auditor may express an unqualified or qualified opinion. In these cases, he is convinced that the dissolution of the company as a going concern is neither imminent nor likely. However, the fact that a company may exhibit some characteristics which are elements of contrary evidence—

such as an accumulated deficit in retained earnings or various financial or operating difficulties—does not automatically lead to the conclusion that an unqualified opinion is not appropriate. In order for this conclusion to be appropriate, these characteristics should be inter-related and have a significant bearing on the company's ability to survive. Normally, both financing and operating problems will be present, and several elements of each type of problem will be apparent.

This chapter deals almost entirely with the going-concern concept as it affects the evidence-gathering aspects of the examination. The effect of the going-concern concept on reporting has two facets. In some cases, the contrary evidence is so compelling that the auditor is convinced that the financial statements prepared on a going-concern basis are not fairly presented. Consequently, an adverse opinion is appropriate. The present criteria used by auditors for the expression of an adverse opinion—including going-concern problems—are explored in the next chapter. The other reporting aspect—report language, including expression of a "piecemeal opinion"—is discussed in the final chapter.

7

Exceptions Based on Lack of Fair Presentation

"Whenever financial statements deviate materially from generally accepted accounting principles, the issuance of a qualified opinion or an adverse opinion is required by the first reporting standard."[1] An adverse opinion is the opposite of an unqualified opinion. In an adverse opinion, the auditor expresses the conclusion that the financial statements taken as a whole *do not* fairly present financial position, results of operations, and changes in financial position in conformity with generally accepted accounting principles. Audit reports expressing an adverse opinion are extremely rare. There is a presumption that at the point when such a report would be issued the auditor would usually either have resigned the engagement or have been dismissed. However, through access to report files of public accounting firms, enough cases were acquired to identify the criteria used in deciding that an adverse opinion should be expressed. These cases also included many qualified opinions for which supporting memoranda indicated why an adverse opinion had not been expressed.

Although the directing concepts of relative magnitude, probability, and utility all have a bearing on the decision to express an adverse opinion, the relative emphasis given to the concepts differs between two distinct categories of exceptions which may lead to an adverse opinion—exceptions stemming from uncertainties and exceptions resulting from a choice by management. Departures from generally accepted accounting principles are involved in both categories, but the cause of the departure is an important consideration in the reporting decision.

---

[1] Statement on Auditing Procedure No. 33, AICPA, New York, 1963, Chapter 10, paragraph 37.

Uncertainty-Related Departures

Within the category of departures from generally accepted accounting principles related to uncertainties, a distinction may be drawn between situations in which the uncertainties are pervasive enough to consider that there is a possibility of imminent liquidation, and situations in which the uncertainty is isolable and liquidation is not considered to be imminent. In other words, in terms of identifying report language, the categories are disclaimer versus adverse, and "subject to" versus "except for."

Disclaimer versus Adverse Opinion. As explained in Chapter 6, the auditor's analysis of pervasive uncertainties surrounding a company's continued ability to operate includes consideration of the impact of possible losses caused by forced liquidation on the financial statements. Uncertainty concerning a company's status as a going concern normally means that financial statements prepared on a going-concern basis evidence a doubt concerning recovery of the carrying amounts of a substantial portion of total assets, liabilities are not stated on an adequate basis or properly classified, and material losses have not been properly recognized. However, it is conceivable that in rare cases, because of asset composition and debt structure, the amounts in the financial statements may all be properly stated at net realizable value in the light of all relevant facts. In such cases, an unqualified opinion may be expressed if the footnotes to the financial statements disclose the uncertainty surrounding the company's survival.

Nevertheless, when the company's status as a going concern is in doubt, there are normally questions concerning asset realization, liability recognition and classification, and loss recognition. When the auditor is reasonably convinced that asset realization will be forced and at levels significantly below carrying amounts, an adverse opinion rather than a disclaimer of opinion is issued.

In all cases reviewed, an adverse opinion was expressed only after a disclaimer of opinion had been issued in previous years. Normally, the departure from generally accepted accounting principles in question was an overvaluation of assets. Stated succinctly, an adverse opinion was expressed when the auditor was convinced that assets *were* substantially overstated; that is, he believed that the statements required correction and he could propose a recommended adjustment.

The following case illustrates a situation in which a disclaimer of opinion was issued for several years. Doubt concerning the company's status as a going concern was not sufficient, without additional experience, for the auditor to conclude that assets were definitely overstated.

111

The company was established in 1962, but production activity was suspended early in 1967, and the company has experienced substantial losses during the past five years, as follows (in millions):

1966	$125
1967	150
1968	75
1969	25
1970	30

Operating figures for the year were insignificant, and the condensed balance sheet at December 31, 1970, (in millions) was as follows:

Assets		Liabilities	
Current.............	$ 55	Current.............	$140
Machinery and equipment, net.........	40	Loans from stockholders	300
Deferred research and development costs, net	325	Capital stock	20
		Deficit, after elimination of $590 million contributed by stockholders	(40)
	$420		$420

Because of the uncertainty of recovery of the costs in inventories, machinery and equipment, and deferred research, we withheld an opinion on the financial statements for the years ended December 31, 1966, 1967, 1968, and 1969. For the year ended December 31, 1970, we decided it was necessary to render an adverse opinion since it has become apparent that there is no reasonable basis to expect any recovery of deferred research and product development costs through either sales of the product rights or through any other potential means of disposition. In addition, the ultimate realizable value on the disposition of machinery and equipment was not determinable but would most likely be less than the carrying value.

Our report, which covered both 1970 and 1969 since comparative statements were given, read as follows:

To the Board of Directors:

We have examined the balance sheets of IAC, Inc. as of December 31, 1970, and 1969, and the related statements of loss *and deficit for the years then ended. Our examinations were made in accordance with generally accepted auditing standards, and accordingly included such tests of the accounting records and such other auditing procedures as we considered necessary in the circumstances.*

Since incorporation, the company has been engaged primarily in developing and improving products in an effort to reach a commercial scale of operation. However, production was suspended in 1967, and research operations for new methods, products, etc., were discontinued in 1969. The unamortized portion of research and product development costs in the amount of $325,000,000 is included in the balance sheet as a deferred charge as of December 31, 1970. The company has represented to us that the value of the patents should cover these costs; however, since the company has not experienced profitable operations to date, and in view of the fact that production has been suspended, it is questionable whether these costs can be recovered in the future.

Specialized machinery and equipment is held for resale and is carried at net depreciated value of $40,000,000 in the accompanying balance sheet as of December 31, 1970. The company's estimated recoverable value is approximately $30,000,000; however, the ultimate realizable value on the disposition of this machinery and equipment depends on circumstances which cannot now be evaluated.

Because of the significance of the matters discussed in the preceding paragraphs, it is our opinion that the accompanying financial statements do not present fairly the financial position of IAC, Inc., as of December 31, 1970 and 1969, or the results of its operations for the two years then ended in conformity with generally accepted accounting principles.

The degree of certainty required concerning overvaluation is indicated by the comment that there was "no reasonable basis to expect any recovery of deferred research and product development costs through . . . any . . . potential means of disposition." Normally, the evidence of overvaluation must be compelling, and the auditor must be able to make a reasonable estimate of the adjustment required—that is, overvaluation is quantifiable.

When the overvaluation can be quantified, the auditor can evaluate the relative magnitude of the misstatement. In the following case, the relative magnitude of overstatement exceeds 100 per cent of net assets.

Pertinent financial data for the DTT Co. as of December 31, 1970, is as shown on the following page.

	(000 omitted)
Current assets	$ 6,150
Current liabilities	6,100
Net current assets	50
Plant and equipment	2,200
Other assets	500
Long-term debt	$(2,200)
Net assets	$ 550

History and Operations

The company had experienced substantial operating losses as follows:

Year Ended May 31	Loss Before Income Taxes (000 omitted)
1970	$1,200
1969	3,200
1968	5,000

Because of the losses experienced in 1968 and 1969 and the question whether the carrying value of certain assets would be realized (together with other matters), we withheld an opinion on the financial statements taken as a whole for each of the years 1968 and 1969. For the year ended December 31, 1970, we gave an adverse opinion on the financial statements since operations continued to be unprofitable and the expected losses on the continued operation or disposition of one division were of such significance that withholding an opinion was not, in our opinion, adequate.

Basis for Adverse Opinion

The sales volume declined dramatically from 1967 to 1970. The sales volume after December 31, 1970, continued to decline, and the company was losing money at a substantial rate. We worked with the company in trying to dispose of this operation, and based upon discussions with prospective buyers and an evaluation of the operation, all indications were that a substantial loss was inherent in the receivables and inventories.

Other than for realization problems, the inventories were stated on a conservative basis. Provision was made for reduced prices because of closeout of specific models, and component parts in excess of forecasted usage were written off. However, even with this conservative valuation, substantial losses were expected since all indications were that the company could not continue to sell these units in any volume *which could be efficiently produced, and the possibility of selling the entire inventory at reduced prices indicated that substantial losses would also be realized.*

We, together with the company, made some estimates of the potential losses which could be realized on the disposition or closing of this operation, and the estimate indicated losses of $600,000 to $800,000 would be incurred. In view of the significance of this indicated loss, and considered in relation to the net assets of the company (stated at $550,000 at December 31, 1970), we concluded that an adverse opinion was required.

The auditor may not always be able to quantify the loss when he is convinced that assets are overvalued. However, he may be able to ascertain that losses will be at least at a given level. In these cases, if the company records a loss at this minimum level, the auditor would then be able to disclaim an opinion rather than express an adverse opinion.

The main source of evidence in concluding that an adverse opinion is more appropriate than a disclaimer of opinion seems to be the passage of time. For this reason, as previously stated, an adverse opinion related to a going-concern problem is normally not expressed unless the company has previously received a disclaimer of opinion. Although it is conceivable that a company's deterioration could be so rapid that the "disclaimer" stage would be passed between report dates, such rapidity is not the norm.

Adversity in the life of a business entity is not unusual. If financing or operating problems occur, the auditor takes note of these factors as evidence which may contradict the going-concern assumption. If the auditor concludes that continuation of the company as a going concern depends on satisfactory resolution of a complex of financing and operating problems and that future resolution of these matters is uncertain, he will disclaim an opinion. With the passage of time, the auditor's experience in observing the company's response to problems may lead him to believe that satisfactory resolution is unlikely. In these cases, he may be convinced that assets definitely are overstated and he will, accordingly, express an adverse opinion unless the overstatement is corrected.

"Subject to" versus "Except for." The same criterion of being convinced of asset overvaluation which applies to the disclaimer versus adverse decision also applies to the "subject to" versus "except for" decision. The only distinction between the two is their origin. For a "subject to" qualification to be appropriate initially, the exception must be isolable so that the continued existence of the entity is not threatened by a potential adverse resolution of the uncertainty.

In the following case, realization of an asset which accounted for approximately one-eighth of total assets and one-third of net assets was uncertain.

Included among the company's assets were certain interests in a secondary oil recovery (waterflood) project consisting of a 50 per cent net profits interest and overriding royalties.

During the years 1962 through 1964, the company did not receive any income on the investment in the net profits interest, and received only a minor amount of income on the overriding royalties. In each of the above years, we received a letter from the operator of the waterflood project. At the year-end 1964, the operator stated that they had still been unable to form an effective "flood bank," but that they were still hopeful that a successful waterflood would be developed. They represented that the project would be continued for at least one additional year.

In view of the operator's letters, we had attempted to have the company amortize its investment in these interests over four years from 1962 through 1965. The company refused, since it felt this would be detrimental to its tax position. The company represented to us that no writeoff of the carrying value should be made since it was believed that the operator's continuation of the project in 1965 demonstrated continued feasibility of the project.

We could not insist that the company amortize the carrying value since we were not in a position to question the operator of the waterflood project; the oil reserves apparently were still in the ground, and, if the project were to be successful, the company's investment could be recovered.

We rendered a "subject to" opinion on realization since we did not have sufficient facts to form an opinion that a clear exception to the 1964 financial statements was called for.

New facts, developed during our 1965 audit, indicated that the ultimate recovery of the cost of the investment in the secondary oil recovery (waterflood) operation ($600,000) was still uncertain; however, it appeared that the carrying value of the investment was overstated since the operator advised us that the best he could hope for would be to recover some of the cash costs previously lost through continued operations and that nothing would accrue to our client's net profits interests. Accordingly, neither continuation of the "subject to" opinion given in 1964 nor issuance of a disclaimer of opinion would be appropriate since we were of the opinion that the financial statements were not fairly presented without adjustment of the investment in this project.

Following is a summary of pertinent financial information as of December 31, 1965 (in thousands):

Assets

Current assets	$ 100,000
Investments	1,600,000
Plant, property, and equipment, net of reserves for depreciation and depletion	700,000
	$2,400,000

Equities

Current liabilities	100,000
Reserve for tax contingencies	500,000
Common stock and paid-in surplus	1,000,000
Retained earnings	800,000
	$2,400,000
Income before taxes	$ 150,000
Net income after provision for tax contingencies	200,000

We believed that the client should provide for a maximum loss on the waterflood properties of $550,000 as of December 31, 1965, because we had doubts as to the company's ability to sustain the tax deduction of loss on sales or other disposition of these properties periodically against operating income. After lengthy discussions, we were unable to convince management that a book reserve would not change the company's tax position.

We carefully weighed the materiality factors involved and the uncertainties as to ultimate loss and tax benefit, if any, to be recovered from loss on sale or disposition. We concluded that a clear exception was appropriate, as opposed to an adverse opinion.

The middle and opinion paragraphs of our 1965 report were as follows:

As described in Note 3 to the financial statements, a substantial portion of the Company's assets at December 31, 1965, is represented by its investment at cost in oil and gas interests ($600,000) relating to secondary oil recovery operations. Based upon presently known facts concerning the secondary recovery project, it does not appear that cost of this investment will be recovered even though the project is still being continued by the oil operator.

In our opinion, except for the effect upon the financial statements of an adjustment to the carrying value of the investment in oil and gas interests, as referred to in the previous paragraph, the accompanying statements present fairly . . . .

Several things are noteworthy about this case. Although the relative magnitude of the asset involved was large—one-third of net assets—no consideration was given to disclaiming an opinion rather than expressing an opinion subject to the uncertain recovery of the investment. Qualitative criteria outweigh relative magnitude in uncertainty situations; since the continued existence of the entity would not be jeopardized by a substantial loss on the investment, a qualified opinion was expressed. When the auditor had sufficient evidence to propose an adjustment to "correct" the financial statements, the exception could no longer be regarded as an uncertainty.

In the illustrated case, once the exception was regarded as a clear departure from generally accepted accounting principles, attention seemed to focus on the relative magnitude of the exception for purposes of distinguishing between an "except for" qualification and an adverse opinion. Since the exception originated as an uncertainty, however, the cause of the exception is attributable primarily to the circumstances rather than to a willful selection by management of an inappropriate presentation in the initial circumstances. The cause of the exception is one of the important qualitative criteria considered in the decision to express an adverse opinion.

Departures Based on Choice

Management's willful choice of an accounting presentation that the auditor believes is not in conformity with generally accepted accounting principles is the situation usually contemplated in discussions of adverse opinions. For this reason it is presumed that the auditor would resign the engagement or be dismissed at the point when an adverse opinion would be expressed. Nevertheless, adverse opinions are expressed after careful consideration of the relevant reporting concepts.

Relative Magnitude. Generally, the relative magnitude of an exception is given far more weight in the decision process leading to an adverse opinion than it is in the decision process leading to a disclaimer of opinion. Not enough cases were reviewed to offer clear quantitative guidelines for the role of relative magnitude in the report-type decision process. However, both the cases reviewed and the discussions with practicing accountants left a clear impression that when the relevant base of comparison relates to financial position, rather than results of operations, the percentage is relatively high—generally 50 per cent or greater.

The following two cases are offered as representative of the decision process involving measures related to financial position. The first case is somewhat unusual in that the company was in the process of liquidation at the start of the audit engagement. However, since the case is a clear illustration of the importance of relative magnitude, it is presented here.

AT Co. was in the process of liquidation at December 3, 1970. In its wind-up process, the company was endeavoring to collect its notes and accounts receivable from customers and former agents; however, significant losses in excess of the company's reserve were expected.

We were engaged to audit the balance sheet only, which at December 31, 1971, was as follows:

Assets

Cash and other assets	$ 50,000
Receivables (less reserve of $100,000)	1,300,000
	$1,350,000

Liabilities

Loan from bank	$2,000,000
Accounts and notes payable and accrued liabilities	500,000
Capital stock	150,000
Accumulated deficit	(1,300,000)
	$ 1,350,000

As can readily be seen, the company's principal asset was its receivables. Since the company had been in the process of liquidation for almost one year, it was possible to compute, with relative certainty, the amount of loss that would be sustained in collection of the receivables. The company estimated and represented to us that the reserve was inadequate by $800,000 (approximately 60 per cent of total assets), and our review indicated this figure was realistic. Management did not wish to provide the reserve at this time partly because of tax consequences. Accordingly, we decided that an adverse opinion was required. The middle and opinion paragraphs of our report read as follows:

> *The Company in its final process of liquidation is endeavoring to fully collect its outstanding notes and accounts receivables; however, in view of the financial difficulties of many of its former agents and customers, it is expected that significant losses will be sustained. The Company estimates that its reserve for losses on*

collection of receivables is insufficient by $800,000.

In view of the significance of the understatement of the reserve for losses on collection of doubtful receivables, in our opinion the accompanying balance sheet does not present fairly the financial position of AT Co. as of December 31, 1971. However, in our opinion, . . . cash, other assets, and liabilities shown therein are fairly stated, in conformity with generally accepted accounting principles applied on a basis consistent with that of the preceding year.

The next case involves an appraisal write-up of assets—one of the most common causes of adverse opinions.

Pertinent financial data as of December 31, 1970, are as follows:

Current assets	$ 250,000
Operating property and equipment,	
net, at cost	100,000
Operating rights and other	
intangibles, at cost	150,000
Appraisal increment assigned to	
operating rights	2,000,000
	$2,500,000
Current liabilities	800,000
Long-term debt	100,000
Common stock	100,000
Deficit	(500,000)
Appraisal surplus	2,000,000
	$2,500,000
Operating revenues	$1,750,000
Net loss	500,000

During 1966, management recorded (over our objections) an appraisal increment of $2,500,000 in operating rights. In the opinion of management, the increment was necessary to properly reflect the value of these operating rights. The increment was recorded net of income taxes that would be applicable in the event of sales of the rights. The company lost $60,000 in 1968, $30,000 in 1969, and $500,000 in 1970.

After a standard scope paragraph, our report read as follows:

The accompanying statement of income (loss) reflects a loss of $500,000 for the year ended December 31, 1970. Losses of $30,000 and $60,000 were reported for the years ended December 31, 1969 and 1968, respectively. Realization of the investment in *operating property and equipment ($100,000) and operating rights ($150,000) and of the appraisal increment assigned to operating rights ($2,000,000) is dependent upon (1) the success of future operation, or (2) the sale or other disposition of the assets for at least these amounts.*

The Company has heretofore followed the practice of carrying operating rights at cost but adopted the practice in 1970 of reporting these rights at an appraised value, reflecting what the Company would expect to receive from their sale, as further described in Note 3. As a result of this change, $2,000,000, representing the excess of appraisal value over cost reduced by applicable income taxes in the event of sale of these rights at appraised value, has been shown in the asset accounts and in appraisal surplus in the capital section of the accompanying balance sheet. Since no amortization is recorded in these rights, there was no effect on the reported income (loss) of the Company.

In view of the materiality of the effect of the above noted change to a practice which we believe is at variance with generally accepted accounting principles, we are of the opinion that the financial statements do not present fairly the financial position. . . .

The appraisal increment in this case accounts for approximately 80 per cent of total assets. With an exception of this magnitude—when a departure from generally accepted accounting principles is involved— the conclusion of the auditor is normally that an adverse opinion is required even though the exception is isolable and its impact on the statements is clear. Thus, in contrast to the treatment of uncertainties, "sufficiently material" means something much closer to the usual connotation of "material."

While the last two cases discussed involved situations in which the impact of the exception was primarily on financial position, the next case illustrates a situation in which the impact is primarily on earnings. The case is limited to the opinion expressed, followed by relevant excerpts from the financial statements.

We have examined the balance sheet of ABC Corp. as of July 31, 1970, and the related statements of earnings (loss) and deficit for the year then ended. Our examination was made in accordance with generally accepted auditing standards, and accordingly included such tests of the accounting records and such other auditing procedures as we considered necessary in the circumstances.

Included in net earnings is a $25,000 gain on sale of assets to an affiliate, as explained in Note 5 to the financial statements. Since collection of the receivable arising from such sale is contingent upon *realization by the affiliate of its remaining cost of such assets, we believe generally accepted accounting principles require that such $25,000 be recorded in a valuation allowance and that this allowance be deducted from the related receivable in the balance sheet.*

Because of the materiality of the effect of the Company's accounting for the transaction described in the preceding paragraph on notes receivable from affiliate, deficit and stockholders' equity and on net earnings, and because we are unable to determine the collectibility of such note receivable from affiliate, we are of the opinion that the financial statements do not present fairly the financial position of ABC Corp. at July 31, 1970, or the results of its operations for the year then ended, in conformity with generally accepted accounting principles.

The financial statements show:

	1970	1969
Note receivable from affiliates (Note 5)	*$140,000*	*$140,000*
Deficit	*(25,000)*	*(50,000)*
Total stockholders' equity	*130,000*	*100,000*
Net earnings (loss)	*30,000*	*(3,000)*

Note 5 is as follows:

During the year the Company took possession of equipment under lease which had a book value of $90,000 plus a receivable of $10,000 for unpaid rentals and expenses. In addition the Company acquired the merchandise inventory of the lessee for a consideration of $75,000. Such equipment, inventory, and receivables were sold to an affiliate for $200,000, a gain of $25,000. The $200,000 note has been reduced to $140,000 through liquidation of a portion of the inventory, and it is expected that the remainder of the inventory and equipment will be sold for an amount in excess of $140,000.

In this case, the incorrect treatment of the gain on the sale of assets to an affiliate accounted for over 75 per cent of the increase in earnings and over 80 per cent of earnings. Thus, the relative magnitude is well over the rough guide of greater-than-50-per cent of the relevant base applied to measures related to financial position. The reason that the auditor did not express an adverse opinion on results of operations and a qualified opinion on the financial position of the company may be attributed to qualitative considerations.

Even though the relative magnitude of the exception is a more direct consideration in the decision to express an adverse opinion than it is in the decision to disclaim an opinion, qualitative criteria still influence the decision process. For example, in one case reviewed, a 16 per cent overstatement of net income resulted in an adverse opinion on results of operations although a qualified opinion was expressed on financial position. On the other hand, in another case, failure to write off obsolete production facilities which accounted for less than 50 per cent of total assets but would have resulted in an extraordinary loss of several times normal earnings resulted in an "except for" qualification on both financial position and results of operations. These cases indicate that several qualitative factors are also given careful consideration in the decision to express an adverse opinion. In addition, the decision to express an adverse opinion is somewhat discretionary; that is, while auditors may feel that errors in excess of a certain percentage necessitate an adverse opinion, such an opinion may be expressed— when the errors do not reach that level—as a means of voicing extreme disapproval of the accounting practice.

Probability. The role of probability in the decision to express an adverse opinion was alluded to in the discussion of the distinction between an adverse opinion and a disclaimer of opinion. In this context, probability refers to "degree of belief" and relates to the quality of evidence available to support a belief. The persuasiveness of evidence required to support an adverse opinion normally is significantly greater than that required for any other type of audit report. The following case highlights the contrast between suspecting an incorrect presentation and knowing that the presentation does in fact necessitate an adverse opinion.

During our December 31, 1970 audit we discovered that apparently in order to reduce income taxes, payments of commissions and salaries of $75,000 (over one-half of operating expenses) had been made to individuals who, so far as we could determine, had rendered no services to the company. These individuals signed receipts for the payments, and the amounts paid or accrued, net of withholding taxes, were turned over to the stockholders and subsequently used to increase the capital stock of the company.

While we were quite certain that no services had been rendered by these individuals, this is not something that we could report as a fact, which we would have to be able to do to render an adverse opinion. Such an opinion could conceivably be challenged on the basis that we could not know what services were, or were not, rendered. The only thing we can be completely sure of is that we were unable to satisfy ourselves as to the services rendered.

This example was specifically chosen to illustrate an extreme. In this case, an adverse opinion would have been tantamount to a charge of serious wrongdoing. Not all situations are this extreme. Expression of an adverse opinion, however, requires very compelling evidence. In one case, this degree of evidence was described as "the conclusive substantive evidence to support an adverse opinion." In another case, the judgment of the auditor was expressed as follows: "We determined that we should not issue an adverse opinion since we are not absolutely certain that the investment will prove worthless and, therefore, cannot say that the financial statements do not present fairly financial position and results of operations."

Utility. Since the auditor is presumed to be an expert in the application of generally accepted accounting principles, he should never pass a judgment on the appropriateness of an accounting principle on to a report reader; the auditor should decide whether an accounting treatment is correct. Consequently, the two elements of the "utility" reporting concept relevant for the decision to express an adverse opinion are the pervasiveness of the exception and the nature of the exception.

Pervasiveness. If a departure from generally accepted accounting principles has such a pervasive impact on the financial statements that an appraisal of the statements in the light of the departure is virtually impossible, a qualified opinion is not justified and an adverse opinion should be expressed. On the other hand, if the exception is isolable and the auditor can quantify the impact of the departure on the financial statements, a qualified opinion is possible.

For departures from generally accepted accounting principles, pervasiveness is generally thought of in terms of the number of financial statement items affected by the incorrect accounting practice. The following case illustrates an exception regarded as isolable and the related reasoning involved. To focus on the single criterion of pervasiveness, no amounts are presented.

Total assets of the company include buildings recorded at new replacement value (insurance appraisal). The land is not recorded. For newer properties, cost is higher than appraisal because of the unrecorded land cost. For the other properties, however, it is impossible to determine the difference.

It was clear that the practice was not generally accepted and that we would have to qualify our report. We explained the practice in a middle paragraph, and the opinion paragraph read, "In our opinion, except for the effect upon the balance sheet and statement of surplus of the method of accounting for land and buildings explained above, the accompanying financial statements present fairly. . . . "

We considered whether an adverse opinion was called for, but concluded that it was not, since the effect was limited to only property and surplus, was clearly disclosed, and therefore in our opinion should not have been misleading to the reader.

The precise number of items which would have to be affected before an adverse opinion would be required cannot be quantified on the basis of the cases reviewed in this study. In addition, the relationship among reporting concepts, such as relative magnitude and pervasiveness, cannot be specified with any degree of precision. Generally, as pervasiveness increases the importance of relative magnitude appears to diminish.

The following case illustrates the upper limit of pervasiveness—virtually every item in the financial statements. Again, to emphasize the reporting criterion under discussion, no amounts are included. Since it contains all relevant matters, only the auditor's report is presented.

ACCOUNTANTS' REPORT
To the Board of Directors
XY Industries, Inc.

We have examined the consolidated balance sheet of X Co., Inc., and subsidiaries (as then constituted and prior to the pooling transaction described in the succeeding paragraph) as of December 31, 1967, and the related statements of income and retained earnings for the year then ended. Our examination was made in accordance with generally accepted auditing standards, and accordingly included such tests of the accounting records and such other auditing procedures as we considered necessary in the circumstances.

On February 29, 1968, X Co., Inc., and Y Co., Inc., combined on a "pooling of interests" basis under the name XY Industries, Inc. The accompanying financial statements do not include the consolidated accounts of Y Co., Inc., which is the predominant constituent of the combined companies. In our opinion, generally accepted accounting principles applicable in these circumstances require the retroactive consolidation of Y Co., Inc., and subsidiaries with X Co., Inc. (now XY Industries, Inc.), and its subsidiaries. The financial statements of Y Co., Inc., for its fiscal year ended June 30, 1967, were examined by other independent public accountants.

In view of the failure to give effect in the accompanying financial statements to the pooling transaction described in the preceding paragraph, it is our opinion that the accompanying financial statements *do not present fairly the consolidated financial position of X Co., Inc., and subsidiaries (now XY Industries, Inc.) at December 31, 1967, or the results of their operations for the year then ended. However, in our opinion, the accompanying consolidated balance sheet and consolidated statements of income and retained earnings do present fairly the financial position of X Co., Inc., and subsidiaries (as then constituted) at December 31, 1967, and the results of their operations for the year then ended, in conformity with generally accepted accounting principles applied on a basis consistent with that of the preceding year.*

The impact of the departure from generally accepted accounting principles would not always have to be as pervasive as is the departure in the previous illustration. For example, a statement of income which presented sales less cost of sales as a net amount would normally be regarded as a departure from generally accepted accounting principles with a *pervasive* impact. However, as the first case in the next section indicates, other reporting criteria may change this judgment.

Nature of Item. The most significant factor considered by the auditor with respect to the nature of the item causing the exception is the intent of management in choosing the accounting presentation. If the intent of management appears to be to mislead readers of the financial statement, an adverse opinion is called for. The adverse opinion is perceived by auditors as a means for expressing a strong disapproval of the financial representations of management.

If the presentation is not the result of a management choice, but results from an external imposition of some type, then management intent may be easily assessed. The following case illustrates a serious departure from generally accepted accounting principles which is outside management's influence.

The statement of consolidated operations shows "Revenues, less related costs (Note 2)." Note 2 contains the following: "During the 1968 fiscal year, the company was granted a classified contract by the Atomic Energy Commission to pursue a research effort in connection with gas centrifuge component development, a program of work somewhat more limited in scope than the one the company was previously engaged in. Because of the classified nature of the project, the company is not permitted under the security regulations of the AEC to disclose, among other things, financial details of the contract. Accordingly, it is not possible for the company to disclose details of revenues and related costs in the statement of operations.

The accountants' report contained the following paragraphs:

> *As explained in Note 2, the Company entered into a research contract with the Atomic Energy Commission during the year ended June 30, 1968. The nature of the project is classified and, under the security regulations of the Atomic Energy Commission, the Company is not permitted to disclose pertinent financial information. Accordingly, it is not possible for the Company to disclose details of revenues and related costs in the statement of operations.*
>
> *In our opinion, except that (for the reason stated in the preceding paragraph) the details of revenues and related costs have not been presented in the statement of operations. . . .*

Normally, a departure from generally accepted accounting principles as pervasive as presenting revenues and related costs as a net amount would result in the expression of an adverse opinion. However, since the presentation was a result of a requirement of an outside agency, management had no options in making the presentation.

In fact, qualified opinions with exception to the accounting methods followed result most frequently from the use of an accounting method required by a regulatory agency. Most of the "except for" qualifications reviewed were on the financial statements of railroads, power companies, and other utilities. The Interstate Commerce Commission, the Federal Power Commission, the Federal Communications Commission, and state commissions and agencies impose accounting methods which are departures from generally accepted accounting principles. Foreign tax laws are a less common, but nevertheless notable, source of outside imposition of incorrect accounting methods.

In short, the absence of management intent is not difficult to determine, but its presence is less apparent. The following case illustrates a circumstance which is indicative of management intent.

In 1967, the company decided to sell shares to the public. 1967 was a bad year for the X industry in general and since the company depends almost exclusively on sales to X companies, profits were substantially reduced. This drop in profits only became known to the company at year end (September 30, 1967), apparently after information had been given to the underwriters to the effect that reasonable profits were expected.

Subsequent to preliminary closing of the books (when the poor results were ascertained), a large number of adjustments were booked, increasing the preliminary profit figure substantially. During the course of our audit, we noted a large number of adjustments which would be required to be booked in order to correct the financial statements. Eight of these adjustments were considered significant in themselves.

Our report contained a description of each problem, and additional background information was supplied in the notes to the financial statements. The net effect of these exceptions was to reduce stated profits by 70 per cent.

In view of the substantial effect on the statement of income as well as the number and variety of exceptions encountered, we decided to give an adverse opinion on the statement of income as a whole and a qualified opinion on the balance sheet and statement of stockholders' equity.

While year-end adjustments are not uncommon, a substantial number, all affecting income in one direction, is a reasonable indication that management is not attempting to achieve the fairest possible presentation.

In some cases, management intent is undisguised, as in the following example.

On October 8, 1971, a major loan agreement was modified to provide for prepayment of the principal balance during 1972 without premium. As a result of this modification, we proposed to classify the entire amount of the note as a current liability as of September 30, 1971, with a complete explanation of the circumstances described in a footnote.

The company recognized the most forthright presentation would be to reflect this obligation as a current liability. However, it declined to use this treatment because of the possible effect on the other lines of credit. Based upon its previous experience, the company felt that banks would tend to look at the balance sheet without further consideration of information in the footnotes and would raise questions which, even though satisfactorily answered, might jeopardize these lines of credit.

It was further reasoned that the smaller, less sophisticated banks would concentrate on the financial statements without due regard to the auditors' report or footnotes. Accordingly, the financial vice-president proposed to classify the liability in accordance with the terms of the loan agreement at September 30, 1971, without regard to the subsequent modification whereby the company committed itself to liquidate this debt before September 30, 1972. This officer discussed the proposed treatment with the loan officer of its principal bank line of credit and received no objection.

The proposed presentation was discussed with us, at which time the arguments were advanced that (1) it conformed with the legal *requirements of the agreement as of September 30, 1967, and (2) the principal bank had not objected to it. We explained that the subsequent event was governing and that despite whatever footnote explanation might be made covering the modification, we had no choice but to take exception to the debt classification if this treatment were followed. There was no merit to the company's arguments either with respect to the technical aspects of the loan requirements at September 30, 1971, or with respect to the indicated acceptance of the presentation by the bank; the bank, although having the line of credit technically open, had not renewed notes payable prior to September 30.*

The foregoing discussions took place well in advance of our report date. The financial vice-president concluded that he would prefer a "bad" audit report to proper balance sheet presentation.

The note was approximately 80 per cent of other current liabilities and classification of the note as current would have changed the current ratio from 2.75:1 to 1.53:1.

Management intent, however, is normally not this blatant. For "management intent" to operate as a reporting criterion, the auditor must be reasonably convinced of its existence. Auditors are qualified to examine financial facts objectively and to express opinions on them, but they are not professionally qualified judges of human character. Consequently, the reporting criterion of management intent does not imply that audit programs contain a procedure that states "review and evaluate management's motivation in choosing accounting methods." This is far from the case. Rather, the criterion operates contingently in much the same fashion as the going-concern assumption.

One of the tentative postulates of auditing proposed by Mautz and Sharaf deals with management intent as follows:

> There is no necessary conflict of interest between the auditor and the management of the enterprise under audit.[2]

As with the postulate concerning enterprise continuity, to entirely release this assumption would make auditing an impossible task. In explanation, Mautz and Sharaf state:

> We must assume, regardless of the rare cases in which management's immediate interests might be opposed, that generally there is no conflict between the auditor and the management of the enterprise under examination.

---

[2]R. K. Mautz and Hussein A. Sharaf, *The Philosophy of Auditing,* American Accounting Association, 1961, p. 42.

At the same time we must face the fact of occasional direct conflict. Hence we postulate no *necessary* conflict as the assumption on which we can most reasonably develop auditing theory.[3]

Thus, the auditor does not actively seek to determine management intent. However, if the auditor believes that management intends the statements to be misleading, that belief has an impact on the reporting decision.

Concluding Remarks

When the auditor is convinced that management's intent in a proposed presentation is to mislead financial statement users, he seriously considers expressing his disapproval of the presentation through expressing an adverse opinion. This does not mean that the absence of management intent completely outweighs relative magnitude as a reporting criterion; however, the qualitative criterion definitely affects the application of the quantitative criterion. Generally, the fact that management has chosen an accounting method with the intention of misleading report readers lowers the relative magnitude necessary for an adverse opinion. Conversely, the outside imposition of an incorrect accounting method creates greater tolerance of the departure. However, the criterion is not applied in the initial decision of whether at least a qualified opinion is required. Generally, the relative magnitude criterion plays a greater role in the decision to express an adverse opinion than it does in the decision to disclaim an opinion.

---

[3] *Ibid.*, p. 45.

8

The Present and Future Implementation of the Fourth Reporting Standard

The fourth reporting standard of the generally accepted auditing standards reads as follows:

> The report shall either contain an expression of opinion regarding the financial statements, taken as a whole, or an assertion to the effect that an opinion cannot be expressed. When an over-all opinion cannot be expressed, the reasons therefor should be stated. In all cases where an auditor's name is associated with financial statements the report should contain a clear-cut indication of the character of the auditor's examination, if any, and the degree of responsibility he is taking.

The purpose of this standard is to prevent financial statement users from being misled on either the extent of the auditor's examination or the responsibility for the statements which he assumes in expressing his opinion.

Presumably, financial statement users attach less credibility to financial statements in correspondence with the degree of qualification indicated in the auditor's report. The degree of qualification that the auditor may apply to his report is measured by a classification system that divides audit reports into four basic categories. The polar positions in this system are: (1) no qualification—an unqualified opinion—which means the statements are reliable and (2) ultimate qualification—an adverse opinion—which means the statements are not reliable; that is, they are misleading.

While the fourth reporting standard clearly describes the essence of the auditor's reporting obligation, implementation of the standard in practice has been impeded by lack of explicit guidance on criteria to be used in classifying a reporting situation in accordance with the professionally defined report categories. Specifically, this monograph is aimed at developing criteria for implementing the fourth standard of reporting when an auditor is faced with the following reporting decisions:

1. The distinction between qualified opinions on the one hand and disclaimers of opinion or adverse opinions on the other.
2. The distinction between a disclaimer of opinion and an adverse opinion in certain cases involving pervasive uncertainties.
3. The appropriate use of the "subject to" introduction for qualified opinions.

A combination of inductive and deductive research methods was used to develop the reporting concepts, or criteria, actually used by auditors in making the report-type decision. The primary source for the reporting concepts was a selection of individual cases which brought reporting criteria to the fore. For example, an opinion qualified subject to an uncertainty which in the next year changed to a disclaimer of opinion based on the same uncertainty represents the sort of reporting situation that highlights the criteria for the distinction between report types.

This chapter reviews and summarizes the reporting criteria developed by the research as reported in Chapters 4, 5, 6, and 7 and sets forth my recommendations for future implementation of the fourth reporting standard based upon the material in all prior chapters and informed personal opinion. An appendix to the monograph relates it to auditing theory, practice, and research in general and recommends future research on audit reporting as well as other auditing topics.

The Criteria Presently in Use

As reflected in Institute pronouncements and public accounting firm manuals, the written expression of the reporting criterion for implementing the fourth standard of reporting is succinctly set forth in paragraph 9 of Chapter 10 of SAP No. 33.

> When a qualification is so material as to negative an expression of opinion as to the fairness of financial statements as a whole, either a disclaimer of opinion or an adverse opinion is required.

This monograph explains the distinction between "material" and "so material" which governs the audit reporting process.

Although "materiality" commonly bears a quantitative connotation of relative magnitude, in practice the distinction between "material" and "so material" is influenced by several qualitative considerations. In fact, once the determination has been made that an exception is material enough to require a qualified opinion, a decision that an adverse opinion or a disclaimer is necessary is influenced primarily by qualitative criteria.

The determination that an unqualified opinion cannot be expressed is based on a judgment that a financial statement exception is material. In this initial step in the decision process, the evaluation is essentially the same as that contemplated in the typical reference to materiality in accounting literature. The determination is based on the quantitative significance of the exception, or its relative magnitude. The relative magnitude of the exception is evaluated by comparing the dollar amount of the item of interest to a relevant basis of comparison, such as net income for the period, normal net income, or total current assets. A qualified opinion is expressed when the dollar impact of an exception on the financial statements is sufficiently large.

The research plan for this monograph did not include establishing limits for this initial determination of materiality. The criteria developed in the monograph are those which become relevant after this first step in the decision process has been taken; that is, when the exceptions evaluated are at least material enough to warrant expression of a qualified opinion.

The exceptions considered in this monograph may be conveniently divided into two categories: (1) exceptions based on uncertainty and (2) exceptions based on lack of fair presentation. An important subdivision of the first category is the going-concern exception.

Exceptions Based on Uncertainty

An auditor evaluates the uncertainty which attaches to the accounting measurements made in the preparation of financial statements by a process of induction relating his past experience to the judgments of management concerning the future. If the probability of the outcome of a material event pertinent to statement presentation as judged by management is, in the auditor's view, abnormal in relation to past events of a similar nature, the auditor has an uncertainty exception. In this sense, "probability" refers to rational, rather than statistical, probability.

The relative magnitude of an uncertainty is never conclusive in determining whether a disclaimer of opinion rather than a qualified opinion should be issued. The potential adjustment to the statements must be combined with an evaluation of probability.

An auditor's evaluation of probability involves the construction of a payoff matrix in which the dollar impact on the financial statements of the various possible outcomes of the event are arrayed against the rational probabilities of each outcome. Normally, probability is classified in categories of qualitative likelihood—such as excellent chance, good chance, average chance, or poor chance—rather than specific numeric probabilities. In many cases, the evaluation may not even be placed in a formal matrix although the logic of the payoff matrix is applied.

In evaluating the uncertainty of the event, the auditor considers the *imminence* of the event and the relevance of past experience as a guide to making a reasonable estimate of the outcome. If the event is not imminent, its remoteness in time reduces its importance with respect to the current financial statements. Relevant past experience to draw on in making the evaluation increases the auditor's confidence in the probability measures.

By combining potential relative magnitude and probability, the auditor determines the expected magnitude of the event, which he then compares to the normal bases of comparison used for assessing materiality. Even at this stage, however, the quantitative impact of expected magnitude is not presumptive in the decision to disclaim rather than qualify.

"Utility" is the primary criterion of whether an auditor should qualify his opinion or disclaim an opinion. The concepts relevant to evaluation of reporting utility are (1) the auditor's *expertise* relevant to the cause of the report exception, (2) the *nature* of the item, and (3) the *pervasiveness* of the item causing the exception.

The expertise reporting concept is presently used to distinguish those reporting situations in which the item causing the exception may be appropriately shifted to the reader of the report for evaluation; therefore, it has a bearing on questions involving the distinction between unusual uncertainties and departures from generally accepted accounting principles. When an auditor issues a qualified opinion or a disclaimer of opinion based upon an uncertainty, the report reader should not reasonably be able to expect the auditor to be capable of evaluating the exception; the exception should fall outside his area of competence or expertise. No audit evidence should exist which the auditor could feasibly obtain to form a judgment on the proper presentation of the item. The sources of feasible evidence include the opinions of other experts, such as attorneys.

The two reporting concepts which bear directly and most importantly on the distinction between an uncertainty qualification and a disclaimer of opinion are the nature and the pervasiveness of the item causing the exception. These two qualitative criteria are paramount in determining that an uncertainty exception is "sufficiently material" to necessitate a disclaimer of opinion.

In present practice, if the nature of the item causing the exception is a general condition rather than a specific, localized problem, the presumption exists that a disclaimer of opinion is appropriate. On the other hand, a qualified opinion is appropriate when the report reader can identify the circumstances giving rise to the qualification and may, in accordance with the expertise criterion, make his own evaluation of the exception. The qualification should direct the reader's attention to a localized problem—a specific exception. In contrast, if the exception relates to a general condition, the report reader is unable to determine clearly how, and to what extent, the reliability of the financial statements is impaired.

Pervasiveness is an important criterion for the evaluation of reporting utility. If the exception permeates the financial statements to such an extent that appraisal of the statements is virtually impossible, a disclaimer of opinion is appropriate. On the other hand, if the exception is isolable and the significance of the impact of the exception on the statements is apparent, a qualified opinion adequately communicates the situation to the report reader.

As reporting concepts are presently applied, the only uncertainties that lead to a disclaimer of opinion are those that imperil the continued existence of an entity. In other words, only going-concern problems typically lead to a disclaimer of opinion.

Going-Concern Exceptions

A well-recognized convention in accounting theory and practice is the assumption that an entity will continue to exist indefinitely in the absence of evidence to the contrary. This convention is commonly referred to as the going-concern assumption, and its practical import is that forced-sale or liquidation values and liquidation commitments are ignored in financial statement preparation. The accounting convention also has an impact on the auditor's examination and report.

Although the auditor does not actively seek to validate the status of the entity as a going concern in the course of his examination, he remains aware of the possibility that the entity is not a going concern. The auditor does not assume that liquidation is impossible, but plans his examination as if the assumption were true. Thus, the going-concern assumption operates contingently as an evidential criterion. The auditor remains alert to any indication that liquidation may be imminent and, if evidence contrary to the going-concern assumption comes to his attention, he makes an evaluation of that evidence.

Contrary evidence usually falls into two broad categories—financing problems and operating problems. Financing problems may be evidenced by a liquidity deficiency, an equity deficiency, debt default, and shortage of funds. Operating problems may be evidenced by continued operating losses, doubtful prospective revenues, factors jeopardizing ability to operate, and ineffective operational control. These problems, in turn, may be mitigated by evidence of probable future operating success or satisfactory resolution of financing needs.

Financing problems may be mitigated by a waiver of default or an anticipated influx of funds, and operating problems may be mitigated by reliable company plans or budgets and essential operational or management changes.

If the auditor concludes on the basis of his evaluation of the contrary evidence and any mitigating factors that there is a substantial and imminent possibility of liquidation, the result is usually substantial uncertainty concerning (1) the recovery of total assets, (2) the classification and basis of liabilities, and (3) the recognition of material losses. In these circumstances, present practice is to disclaim an opinion on the financial statements unless the auditor is convinced that the statements require correction and he can propose a recommended adjustment.

The mere presence of some elements of contrary evidence does not automatically lead to a disclaimer of opinion. Mitigating evidence may partially offset the contrary evidence and reduce the exception to an isolable uncertainty, or the contrary evidence may be completely countered.

Exceptions Based on Lack of Fair Presentation

In the decision process leading to an adverse opinion, the relative magnitude of the exception assumes more importance than for exceptions based on uncertainty. When the relevant base of comparison relates to financial position, if the dollar impact of the departure from generally accepted accounting principles is extremely large, an adverse opinion is usually considered appropriate. When the relevant basis of comparison relates to results of operations, a lower relative magnitude may lead to an adverse opinion. In addition, expression of an adverse opinion is somewhat discretionary. Although an exception which exceeds a certain relative magnitude may necessitate an adverse opinion, the auditor may express an adverse opinion to voice an extreme disapproval of an accounting practice at a lower level of relative magnitude.

Although qualitative criteria are of relatively less importance in evaluating departures from generally accepted accounting principles, they do have a definite impact on the decision process. The quality of evidence necessary to support an adverse opinion must usually be more persuasive than that required for other audit reports. Normally the auditor has sufficient evidence to propose an adjustment which would "correct" the financial statements. The two other qualitative criteria of importance are the pervasiveness of the exception and management's intent in the choice of accounting principles.

Generally, the more pervasive the impact of the exception on the financial statements, the lower the relative magnitude necessary for the expression of an adverse opinion. For departures from generally accepted accounting principles, pervasiveness is generally thought of in terms of the number of financial statement items affected by the incorrect accounting practice. On the other hand, an auditor may express a qualified opinion if his qualification erases the misimpression created by the financial statements as presented and dispels the impact of the incorrectly reported earnings figure.

When the auditor is convinced that management's intent is to mislead statement users, he should seriously consider expressing an adverse opinion. On the other hand, the outside imposition of an incorrect accounting method creates greater tolerance of the departure. The auditor's evaluation of management intent operates contingently. The auditor does not actively seek to determine management intent. He generally assumes that no conflict exists between management and himself concerning a desire for fair presentation, but remains alert to evidence which may contradict this assumption.

Reporting Objectives

In addition to following specific reporting criteria, auditors have several general objectives in mind when writing reports. These general objectives are: (1) equity, (2) communication, and (3) awareness of the reporting environment. The auditor should attempt to balance the advantages and disadvantages of various forms of audit reports to the diverse groups of people who have an interest in audit reports. The audit report must be more than literally truthful. Since an audit report is concise, abstract, and one-way, the auditor should carefully consider the impression likely to be drawn by the reader. Finally, the auditor should consider the reporting environment and, consequently, attempt to achieve uniformity of report language. He may also include certain information in his report to comply with regulatory agency requirements.

Recommendations for Future Implementation

In the process of studying the reporting criteria used by auditors in preparing reports and particularly in surveying the historical development of the criteria as reflected in Institute pronouncements, it became apparent that reporting practice could be improved by changing the requirements for report format as well as by codifying more explicit criteria. Consequently, the recommendations for future implementation of the fourth reporting standard are divided between recommendations as to form and recommendations as to criteria.

Recommendations as to Form[1]

Most of the recommendations as to form concern the format of qualified opinions. When the auditor qualifies his opinion, he expresses a positive opinion on the financial statements taken as a whole, but excludes from that opinion a particular aspect of the financial statements. The qualification explains that, other than the matter described in the qualification, the financial statements are fairly presented in conformity with generally accepted accounting principles.

Middle Paragraph. When the auditor expresses a qualified opinion, the report should always contain one or more paragraphs describing the reason for the qualification and the impact of the qualification on the financial statements. The impact on the statements should be quantified unless the impact is not reasonably determinable—in which case the report should state the inability to quantify the qualification.

Consequently, a qualified opinion should be in the format of a scope paragraph followed by one or more paragraphs describing the qualification, and then the opinion paragraph.

Although the audit report may refer to a note to the financial statements related to the qualification, reference to the note should not be a substitute for a description in the audit report of the matter discussed in the note. Thus a qualified report with a standard scope paragraph followed by an opinion paragraph which stated, "In our opinion, subject to the matter described in Note H, the financial statements . . . " would not be acceptable.

Naturally, when the qualification is based upon a limitation on the scope of the examination, the matter should not be discussed in notes to the financial statements since the statements are the representations of the company, not the auditor.

Qualification Location. All qualified opinions other than those qualified as to consistency should have the qualifying phrase located in the same position in the opinion paragraph. The most noticeable, and therefore desirable, position for the qualifying phrase is the beginning of the opinion paragraph. Consequently, except for consistency exceptions, all qualified opinions should be introduced in the opinion paragraph by the qualifying phrase. The qualifying phrase should refer to the prior descriptive paragraph(s) which explains the reason for the qualification.

The qualifying phrase should begin with the words of qualification, such as "except for." General words of introduction, such as "in

---

[1] Recommendations as to form do not apply to reference to other auditors as described in SAP No. 45 since this reference is not an opinion qualification.

view of the above" or "with the above explanation," are not forceful
enough to indicate qualification.

Rationale of Format Specifications. Requirements of report
layout or topography introduce a certain rigidity into report writing.
Some accountants may believe that their professional judgment is
impeded by such requirements. These requirements, however, are
unrelated to the decision process in reporting and come into effect only
after the auditor has made the decision to express a qualified opinion;
the decision process—the most important area of professional judgment—is not changed.

The proposed requirements on report format may be viewed as a
natural development in the increasing standardization of reporting
described in Chapter 2. In addition, two guiding concepts of reporting—communication and environment—justify uniformity as a desirable
objective of reporting.

To achieve communication with report users, every device
available to the auditor should be used. An additional paragraph(s)
added to the report has a visual impact on the reader. He is alerted that
the report is different from the usual two-paragraph report which
commonly expresses the auditor's approval of the financial statements.
The qualifying phrase at the beginning of the opinion paragraph
reinforces the visual impression; unmistakably, the auditor does not
intend to express approval of all aspects of the financial statements.
Report users cannot be expected to understand a large number of
technical nuances in report language, and uniformity of report format is
a simple means of improving communication.

In addition, the auditor's report should be a self-contained
expression of his conclusions concerning the financial statements; it
should stand by itself as an explanation of the auditor's opinion on the
statements. The auditor's report is his representation fulfilling his
reporting obligation to the reader; management's representations are
contained in the financial statements and footnotes. The auditor's
representations should be clearly conveyed by his report, and the report
reader should not be required to refer to management's representations
to understand the nature of the auditor's qualification. Consequently,
the auditor should explain in his report why he is unable to express a
positive opinion on all aspects of the financial statements.

Since the degree of responsibility assumed by the auditor is
significantly changed when he adds qualifying language to his report,
the form of that qualifying language should unequivocally express the
intended qualification of the financial statements. With so much
importance attached to so few words, there is little justification for
differences in language or form not required by differences in the

underlying circumstances being reported upon. A qualified opinion should be easily distinguishable from the standard form of an unqualified opinion. There should be no doubt about the intent of a qualifying phrase. Any possible confusion between qualification and mere explanation should be eliminated.

Explanatory Disclosures. The mandatory use of one or more middle paragraphs for qualified opinions might cause confusion between this use of the middle paragraph and middle paragraphs not intended to qualify the opinion. SAP No. 33, Chapter 10, paragraph 43, sanctions the use of a middle paragraph without qualification:

> There may be instances where the independent auditor may wish to include in his report additional explanatory matter (which is not required for adequate disclosure) to highlight certain circumstances or to aid in the interpretation of the financial statements. Since such additional disclosure is not intended to qualify the scope of examination or the opinion on the statements, no reference thereto should be made in the opinion paragraph of the independent auditor's report.

The most common use of the nonqualifying middle paragraph is to meet certain reporting requirements of the SEC. An auditor whose report is filed with the SEC may be required to include one or more of three matters in his report even though his opinion is unqualified. The three matters are: (1) changed conditions which necessitate accounting changes and thereby affect comparability, but which do not involve changes in accounting principles employed, (2) material differences between the accounting principles and practices reflected in the financial statements and those reflected in the accounting records, and (3) major inadequacies in the company's accounting system.

Since reports filed with the SEC must include these explanatory disclosures, some auditors include the same report in annual reports or other public distributions. By so doing, the auditor avoids having two different reports on essentially the same financial statements, both of which are available to the public.

In addition to reports to the SEC, the explanatory middle paragraph is sometimes used to describe an unusual aspect of the operations or accounting system of the company reported on. For example, reports on the financial statements of gaming casinos and of nonprofit organizations deriving substantial revenue from voluntary contributions have frequently contained middle paragraphs explaining that receipts are not subject to prerecording control.[2]

Since the existence of a dual use for middle paragraphs has not

---

[2]For a related discussion see D. R. Carmichael, "Auditing and Reporting for Casinos," *The Journal of Accountancy*, February 1972, pp. 71-73.

created insurmountable problems in the past, a requirement for mandatory use of a middle paragraph should not create any new problems. If the visual impact of three paragraphs serves to alert the reader and results in a more careful reading of the report, that reaction would appear to be compatible with use of the middle paragraph for important explanations. However, the possibility of confusing an explanation and a qualification should not be ignored entirely.

If only one use of the middle paragraph were considered acceptable, its use in qualified opinions would seem to have more merit than retaining it as a device for mere explanation.

One solution—and the one recommended here—is to relegate all explanations which are not intended to qualify the opinion to a position after the opinion paragraph. In this manner, a distinction could be drawn between a qualification and an explanation on the basis of the location of the paragraph. In addition, placing the explanatory paragraph after the expression of the opinion avoids the implication that the explanation is necessary for a fair presentation of the financial statements.

Adverse Opinions and Disclaimers. The current format for adverse opinions and disclaimers of opinion normally contains one or more middle paragraphs describing the reasons for the type of report issued, and a final paragraph introduced by a direct reference to the preceding explanation. An important consideration in the language used to express an adverse opinion is that it not resemble the normal expression of an unqualified opinion. In this respect, no changes in present practice seem necessary.

Summary and Example. The following recommendations for changes in the reporting requirements for qualified opinions are offered:

1. A qualified opinion should always contain one or more middle paragraphs describing the reason for the qualification and the impact on the financial statements.
2. The qualifying phrase in the opinion paragraph should be the first phrase in the paragraph and should be introduced by qualifying words.
3. Explanatory paragraphs that are unrelated to a qualification of the opinion paragraph should follow that paragraph.

A qualified opinion prepared in accordance with these recommendations, in which the qualification relates to prior-year federal income taxes, might contain middle and opinion paragraphs worded as follows:

> Although the proceeds of sales are collectible on the installment basis over a five-year period, revenue from such sales is recorded in full by the Company at time of sale, as described more fully in Note 1 to the financial statements. However, for income tax purposes, income is reported only as collections are received, and no provision has been made for income taxes on installments to be collected in the future, as required by generally accepted accounting principles. If such provisions had been made, net income for 1971 would have been reduced by $ _____; retained earnings as of December 31, 1970 and 1971, would have been reduced by approximately $ _____ and $ _____ , respectively; and the balance sheet at December 31, 1971, would have included a liability for deferred income taxes of approximately $ _____ .
>
> Except for the effect on the financial statements of the failure to provide for deferred income taxes as described in the foregoing paragraph, in our opinion the accompanying financial statements present fairly . . . .

Recommendations as to Criteria

The following recommendations should be viewed in historical perspective. Many of the present reporting requirements have been in effect for only ten years; only twenty years ago an auditor was never required to disclaim an opinion.

Most of the recommendations are logical extensions of the trends in reporting described in Chapter 2; some, however, are radical departures from past directions.

"Subject to" or "Except for." The relationship between the "subject to" form of qualification and unusual uncertainties is an artificiality created by SAP No. 32. Historically, before 1962, "subject to" and "except for" were used interchangeably for all types of qualified opinions. The administrative policy of the SEC, established in ASR No. 90, of accepting "subject to" qualifications has caused that phrase to assume unusual importance.

A careful review of reporting practices creates the impression that entirely too much significance is attached to these two words. Consequently, I recommend that the distinction between different types of introductory words for qualified opinions be abandoned. All qualified opinions should be introduced by the introductory words "except for." The middle paragraph of the qualified opinion should be used· to set forth the reason for the qualification. By descriptive wording in the middle paragraph, the auditor should indicate (1) whether he believes the statements are incorrect because they do not reflect an adjustment he has proposed or (2) whether he does not know what adjustments of the statements might be required. The emphasis in reporting should be on the reason for the qualification. With the emphasis removed from the two-word introduction, attention should focus on the description of the qualification.

Since accountants are familiar and reasonably comfortable with the present distinction between "subject to" and "except for" qualifications, the idea of abandoning the "subject to" form is, no doubt, foreign and easily rejected as an initial reaction. However, the evolution of report categories shows gradual and incremental changes. The elimination of "subject to" as an acceptable introduction to the qualifying phrase is a logical step in the development of reporting criteria.

Before SAP No. 32 assigned the current designated meanings to the two forms of qualification, reporting practice was chaotic in the use of the two forms. Either "subject to" or "except for" could be used at the whim of the reporting auditor. At that time, attention naturally focused on drawing a distinction between the two forms and supplying criteria to rationalize the choice of introductory words.

Another decade has passed, and reevaluation of the two forms of qualification is in order. "Subject to" is more ambiguous than "except for" and not nearly as forceful. The "except for" language more clearly conveys an intent to qualify the opinion; if the item mentioned is excluded, the statements are fairly presented. All qualifications are essentially the same in this respect. The auditor's intention is to *except* something from his otherwise positive opinion on the statements.

Any need to distinguish between unusual uncertainties and departures from generally accepted accounting principles can be met by descriptive wording. Reducing the significance of the introductory words should refocus the emphasis where it belongs—on the reason for the qualification.

For example, the following report illustrates a qualification that under present practice would be introduced by "subject to" which is prepared in accordance with the recommendations made in this monograph.

(Standard scope paragraph)

(Middle paragraph)

As is more fully discussed in Note 1 to the financial statements, the Company is presently contesting deficiencies in consolidated Federal income taxes proposed by the Internal Revenue Service for the years 1970 and 1971 in the aggregate amount of $ ____, exclusive of interest. The issue in question is one on which there are conflicting Federal Court decisions and on which further litigation may be required; consequently, it is impossible to determine the extent of the Company's liability, if any, at this time, and no provision has been made therefor in the accompanying financial statements.

(Opinion paragraph)
Except for such adjustments, if any, to accrued Federal income taxes and retained earnings which may result from the final determination of the Company's income tax liability for prior years, as discussed in the preceding paragraph, in our opinion the accompanying financial statements present fairly . . . .

No report reader should be confused by this qualification. The recommended form of reporting actually places less burden on the report reader since he is not expected to recognize the technical nuance which attaches special significance to differing introductory words.

For contrast, the previously illustrated report is presented again, only this time as it might appear under present criteria.

(Standard scope paragraph)

(Opinion paragraph)
In our opinion, subject to the matter discussed in Note 1, the accompanying financial statements present fairly . . . .

Although this example is written to illustrate an extreme, it is not uncommon. Abandonment of the special significance of the "subject to" phrase should have a salutary impact on the writing of qualified opinions.

Disclaimers of Opinion. Only the criteria for disclaimers of opinion based on uncertainty are considered in these recommendations. In addition, pervasive uncertainties which imperil the continued existence of the company are unique and important enough to warrant separate recommendations. Consequently, recommendations related to questions of the going-concern status of a company are treated separately.

Present reporting practice indicates that auditors generally do not believe that an isolable uncertainty, even though of extremely large relative magnitude, should lead to a disclaimer of opinion unless it imperils the continued existence of the company. The decision to disclaim an opinion because of an uncertainty is not based on an isolated consideration of relative magnitude.

In other words, practice contradicts one possible interpretation of paragraph 47, Chapter 10, of SAP No. 33, which states, in part, that:

In some instances where the outcome of a matter is uncertain, the amount may be so material that a qualified opinion is inappropriate.

If "material" is interpreted as relative magnitude, this paragraph does not reflect all important reporting criteria. Consequently, pronouncements of the Committee on Auditing Procedure should be clarified to preclude the possibility of such an interpretation.

The historical development of the fourth reporting standard presents a logical basis for the rejection of a criterion that would require a disclaimer of opinion for an isolable uncertainty of large magnitude.

Originally, the idea of a disclaimer of opinion was closely identified with scope restrictions. In this context, a disclaimer had a natural meaning; if the auditor had gathered so little evidence about the financial statements that he was not in a position to express an informed opinion on them, he should withhold an opinion. To communicate this to report readers, a reporting standard was adopted by the profession to require a clear disclaimer of opinion.

Thus, a third report category was created. An auditor might express an unqualified opinion, but if he had not satisfied himself about a particular financial statement item he would express a qualified opinion excluding that item from his opinion. In a more extreme situation, when his examination was more severely restricted, he would disclaim an opinion. The fourth standard of reporting, therefore, created the idea that qualifications might vary in degree, with a disclaimer of opinion implying the ultimate degree of qualification.

Subsequently, the idea of degrees of qualification was extended to apply to other types of qualified opinions that auditors issued. A restricted examination, however, is a very tangible type of qualification—one that is easily comprehended in a physical sense. When his examination is restricted, either by the client or the circumstances of a particular audit, the auditor does not apply certain auditing procedures. These procedures are physical actions which the auditor has previously experienced performing. Even though in a particular case he cannot perform the procedures—because necessary records have been destroyed or were not kept, or because of timing problems the client activity to which the procedures are ordinarily applied has already passed—the auditor knows that procedures exist which would otherwise provide the necessary evidence.

In contrast, with a major uncertainty the auditor is similarly faced with a lack of evidence, but the cause of that lack of evidence is significantly different. No known auditing procedures could be applied to obtain the necessary evidence. Application of the ultimate degree of qualification—a disclaimer—to this type of situation is highly artificial.

Since the auditor has no special expertise which equips him to evaluate the uncertainty, it is appropriate for him to pass that judgment on to the report reader by qualifying his opinion. The qualification alerts the report reader to the contingency and allows him to make the necessary subjective evaluation concerning the uncertainty.

In these circumstances, the report reader is better served by a qualified opinion which tells him that except for the uncertainty the auditor believes the statements are fairly presented. After performing an unrestricted examination, the auditor should have significant conclusions concerning the conformity of the financial statements with generally accepted accounting principles which he should express in a positive opinion. In these circumstances, a qualified opinion achieves the greatest reporting utility.

Adverse Opinions. In contrast to the auditor's lack of expertise in the area of uncertainties, he is an expert in the application of generally accepted accounting principles. Consequently, the auditor should never pass on to the reader of his report a judgment on the acceptability of the accounting principles applied.

The judgments which the auditor should make include the determination of whether the financial statements taken as a whole are fairly presented in conformity with generally accepted accounting principles. Thus, the category of adverse opinions should be retained.

Although less important than quantitative criteria in the decision process leading to an adverse opinion, qualitative criteria are still a significant factor in that decision process. Consequently, these qualitative criteria should be recognized in Institute pronouncements.

Despite the general recognition of certain percentage relationships in applying the relative magnitude criterion, sufficient evidence is not available to establish quantitative guidelines at the profession level. Consequently, no recommendations are offered for the quantification of "sufficiently material."

Piecemeal Opinions. Chapter 2 traces the development of piecemeal opinions in some detail. Piecemeal opinions were formally introduced as a recognized type of audit report at the same time that the requirement to specifically disclaim an opinion was adopted in 1949. After several decades of practice allowing reports tailored to the circumstances of an engagement, the requirement for a categorical disclaimer of opinion no doubt seemed harsh, and there was a desire to reduce the impact of the requirement and avoid casting unwarranted aspersion on the statements by means of a consolatory piecemeal opinion.

At approximately the same time that piecemeal opinions were introduced, an article in *The Journal of Accountancy* explicitly acknowledged that allowing the issuance of piecemeal opinions appropriately balanced the needs of the client with the protection of third parties.[3] However, over twenty years have passed since then, and the

---

[3] Carman G. Blough, "Significance of Auditing Statement No. 23," *The Journal of Accountancy*, March 1951, p. 395.

auditor must now function to a far greater extent in the public sphere. Reporting requirements based on more or less private relationships between the auditor and his client have little continuing significance.

SAP No. 46, "Piecemeal Opinions," has prohibited the use of that type of report in conjunction with disclaimers of opinion based on client-imposed restrictions. Paragraph 5 states:

> A piecemeal opinion should not be expressed, if, as a result of restrictions imposed by the client (such as not being permitted to examine a sufficient number of subsidiaries of a holding company, not being permitted to observe physical inventories, etc.), the auditor is unable to examine evidence supporting financial statement items or is prevented from applying auditing procedures he believes would be necessary to support an unqualified or qualified opinion on the financial statements taken as a whole.

Thus, piecemeal opinions are now precluded in the very reporting situation which initially gave rise to their recognition.

Piecemeal opinions should be eliminated as a *general* report category and permitted only in specific situations explicitly identified by the Committee on Auditing Procedure, such as the exemptions to the general rule in paragraph 5 identified in SAP No. 46.

One reason for the adoption of the piecemeal opinion was to avoid any implication that the auditor was aware of facts that would discredit the financial statements, but was not disclosing the information because he disclaimed an opinion for other reasons. Since an adverse opinion declares that the auditor believes the financial statements are not fairly presented, he should have no reason to accompany it with a piecemeal opinion.

If the previous recommendation concerning isolable uncertainties of large magnitude is followed, disclaimers of opinion will not be issued in which the uncertainty relates to only one or a few financial statement items. Since this category of disclaimers is the one which most justifies the expression of a piecemeal opinion, there would be little need to continue piecemeal opinions as a general report category.

Elimination of piecemeal opinions as a general report category should be a definite step forward in improving the communication aspect of audit reports. Realistically, it is nearly impossible to explain the difference between a qualified opinion in which one account is excluded from the opinion, and a piecemeal opinion in which all accounts but one are enumerated. Although situations seldom arise in which the contrast between the two types of reports would be that great, the extreme situation highlights the illogic inherent in the piecemeal opinion report category.

When piecemeal opinions were first recognized as a report category, their existence was probably justified by practical and social factors of the time. However, the report category has lingered on past the time of its justification for existence.

Going-Concern Problems. Recommendations for reporting on going-concern problems are more difficult and are expressed with less conviction than previous recommendations.

Chapter 6 outlines the framework used by auditors in deciding whether a disclaimer of opinion is appropriate when a company is faced with the pervasive uncertainties associated with going-concern problems. Although this explanation of the decision framework is considerably more informative than the terse criterion contained in paragraph 47, Chapter 10 of SAP No. 33, it remains vague, and variations in applying the guidelines in practice can be expected. For isolable uncertainties, even those of extremely large magnitude, the recommendation was made that, with adequate financial statement disclosure, a qualified opinion accurately and informatively conveys the auditor's conclusions concerning the financial statements. From this recommendation one can question whether a qualified opinion might not also be sufficient for financial statements affected by pervasive uncertainties, unless the auditor is convinced that the going-concern basis is definitely not appropriate—in which case he would express an adverse opinion.

Before considering the pros and cons of this proposition, a few pertinent, special problems raised by Accounting Series Release No. 115 should be considered, since auditors commonly think of this release when the discussion turns to going-concern problems. ASR No. 115 applies to companies in the operating stage[4] that attempt to raise capital through a public stock issue and, therefore, file a registration statement under the Securities Act of 1933. The release established guidelines for the type of audit report the SEC will accept in a 1933 Act filing for companies exhibiting going-concern problems. As expressed in the final paragraph of the release:

> The Commission has concluded that a registration statement under the 1933 Act will be considered defective because the certificate does not meet the requirements of Rule 2-02 of Regulation S-X when the accountant qualifies his opinion because of doubt as to whether the company will continue as a going concern. The Commission does not intend to preclude companies with pressing financial problems from raising funds by public offerings of securities. It does, however, believe it clear that an accountant's report cannot meet the certification requirements of the 1933 Act unless the registrant can arrange its financial affairs so that the immediate threat to continuation as a going business is removed. The independent accountant must

---

[4] In other words, it does not apply to Article 5A statements of companies in the development stage.

be satisfied that it is appropriate to use conventional principles and practices for stating the accounts on a going concern basis before a registration statement under the 1933 Act can be declared effective.

Thus, if the opinion is qualified or disclaimed, the auditor's report will not meet the SEC's certification requirement.

The SEC issued ASR No. 115 because it was troubled by "bail-out" situations in which the creditors or original shareholders would receive substantially all the proceeds of the stock offering. In this case, the continued existence of the company would still be in doubt even if the offering was successful. In effect, ASR No. 115 requires the auditor to evaluate the financing needs and compare these needs with the use of proceeds disclosed in the prospectus to determine if the amount of capital to be raised will alleviate the immediate threat to continued existence. The auditor's evaluation of financing needs is essentially the same process as the consideration of mitigating factors discussed in Chapter 6. The auditor would consider the company's plans and projections and the data on which they are based.

If the auditor believes that mitigating factors counter the contrary evidence that caused him to question the company's status as a going concern in the first place, he need only arrive at a satisfactory conclusion concerning the acceptability of the underwriting for the report to meet the requirements of the SEC. If adequate funds are contemplated by the underwriting, either a firm underwriting or an "all-or-nothing" underwriting will be acceptable. On the other hand, a "best-effort" underwriting would not be acceptable since the amount to be raised is uncertain and cannot be evaluated in comparison with the use of proceeds. In the case of an "all-or-nothing" underwriting, the audit report would fill a special purpose. If all the stock is sold, then presumably adequate financing would be obtained. However, if less than all is sold, the proceeds would be returned to the subscribers, and no investor would suffer a loss.

Some auditors use a rule of thumb that they should "be in a position to determine that, before certifying to the financial statements, that the company, with the additional financing, as contemplated by the Registration Statement, will be a viable entity for one year from the report date."[5] However, because of unforeseen developments, the entity's existence may be terminated and the auditor can never guarantee a company's continued existence. The essence of the obligation imposed on the auditor by the SEC is his assurance that a comparison of financing needs and the use of proceeds disclosed in the prospectus does not indicate a "bail-out" situation.

---

[5] James I. Konkel, "The Auditor's Responsibility in Filings by Companies That Have a Loss Record," *The CPA Journal*, January 1972, p. 73.

Any contemplated change in reporting criteria for qualified opinions and disclaimers based on uncertainty would not seem to require a change in the position taken by the SEC in ASR No. 115. In fact, the reason underlying its position seems to be an inability in some cases to distinguish between a disclaimer of opinion and a qualified opinion based on the uncertainty of the company's status as a going concern. Abandonment of the distinction would place a greater burden on the quality of the description of the situation in the middle paragraphs of the report, but this problem would arise even if ASR No. 115 had not been issued.

There are two major arguments for retaining the disclaimer report category for uncertainties which imperil the continued existence of a company. First, conveying the situation in descriptive language in a qualified opinion would be extremely difficult. Second, the auditor should in most cases be in a position to make a much more competent evaluation of the situation than the report reader.

Conveying the situation in a qualified opinion would be difficult because the uncertainty is a general condition rather than a localized and specific problem. Naturally, a general condition is more difficult to describe. While the auditor can describe specific aspects of the condition, such as the fact that current liabilities exceed current assets or that the company has had a series of operating losses, it is not the specific elements themselves that are important, but the way that they interrelate and cast a cloud over the validity of substantially all of the data in the financial statements. The uncertainty is pervasive and permeates the financial statements; consequently, it is difficult for the auditor to identify a specific aspect of the financial statements and exclude that aspect from his opinion. The reader of the report cannot determine that a portion of the financial statements is excluded from the opinion and that all other items are fairly presented.

A review of the type of evidence considered by the auditor in evaluating going-concern problems, as described in Chapter 6, indicates that many elements of that evidence may not be available to the report reader. Company plans and projections, the significance of management changes, the effectiveness of control over operations, and knowledge of management's objectivity and knowledgeability are all matters considered by the auditor which would ordinarily not be available to report readers. While the auditor cannot predict the future, he is in a far better position to evaluate the present than any other outsider.

On the other hand, the utility of the disclaimer of opinion to financial statement users is subject to question, and the arguments against retaining the disclaimer category all stem from its questionable utility.

A disclaimer based on an uncertainty is considerably different from a disclaimer caused by a restricted examination. After performing an unrestricted examination utilizing all his professional skills, the auditor whose disclaimer is caused by an uncertainty is in the illogical position of stating that he has no conclusions concerning the statements: In the vernacular which might be used by an average layman—"all that auditing and you can't tell me anything?"

Yet, the auditor has answers to significant questions about the financial statements. Were the statements prepared in conformity with generally accepted accounting principles insofar as was possible? Have the items affected by the uncertainties been stated in conformity with generally accepted accounting principles in all respects other than those contingent on the outcome of the uncertainties? If the uncertainties were removed, would the auditors be able to express an unqualified opinion? An auditor, when issuing a disclaimer, is aware of the obligation to state all his material reservations about the financial statements; but the reader of a disclaimer cannot be expected to fully recognize this obligation.

Implicit in a disclaimer is the assumption that financial statements clouded by uncertainties are useless. This assumption is contradicted by the accepted and expected practice that companies will publish their financial statements. No one suggests that a company whose financial statements are clouded by uncertainties should, in consequence, refrain from issuing financial statements. Rather, we expect the company to issue its statements and, in doing so, to disclose as fully as possible the nature and significance of the uncertainties.

Finally, there is the danger that a disclaimer may be a "self-fulfilling prophecy." If the lack of a positive opinion on a company's financial statements prevents it from raising capital, the report may be a critical factor in the company's demise.

The alternative courses of action are:

1. Eliminate disclaimers for all material uncertainties and have all such exceptions result in qualified opinions.
2. Construct a specially worded report for pervasive uncertainties which includes assurances about conformity with generally accepted accounting principles.
3. Allow pervasive uncertainties to result in disclaimers and combine this position with an educational campaign to indicate the value of the report.

The first position gives full weight to the utility argument, while the last gives full weight to the opposing arguments. The middle, and recommended, position attempts a compromise.

The final paragraph of a report prepared in accordance with the recommendation might read as follows:

> While we believe the accompanying financial statements have been prepared in conformity with generally accepted accounting principles applicable to a going concern, the foregoing matters, the effect of which cannot be determined at this time, give rise to material uncertainties with regard to the future of the Company as a going concern and, as a consequence, to the continued appropriateness of financial statements prepared in conformity with generally accepted accounting principles applicable to a going concern. Accordingly, we are not in a position to, and do not express an opinion on, the accompanying financial statements taken as a whole.

If this alternative were adopted, standard wording for the final paragraph would have to be uniformly followed. The report language must achieve a delicate balance between giving positive assurances to achieve reporting utility and conveying the significance of the uncertainty surrounding the company's continued existence.

Summary. The following recommendations are offered for changes in the reporting criteria for various types of audit reports:

1. The present distinction between "subject to" and "except for" qualifications should be abandoned, and all qualifications should be introduced by phrases using "exception" language, such as "except for."

2. Descriptive wording in a middle paragraph should explain the reason for the qualification.

3. A qualified opinion, rather than a disclaimer of opinion, should be used for exceptions caused by isolable uncertainties, even those of extremely large magnitude.

4. Uncertainties pervasive enough to imperil the continued existence of an entity should lead to a specially worded report giving positive assurance on conformity with generally accepted accounting principles, yet disclaiming a conclusion on the applicability of those principles to the entity.

5. Piecemeal opinions should be prohibited as a general report category.

6. Pronouncements on reporting should recognize the qualitative criteria included in the broad criterion "sufficiently material."

Future Directions for Auditing Research*

In mid-1969 the AICPA's auditing research program was officially launched.[1] For three years I have attempted to plan and initiate a program to provide the Committee on Auditing Procedure, the Institute membership, and others interested in the advancement of auditing theory and practice with evidence and information useful in reaching sound decisions on auditing problems. A numbered series of monographs has been authorized, and additional staff have been devoted to the effort. We are also beginning to contract for studies by outside researchers. Since we firmly believe that a researcher should have his own independent commitment to a project, we would prefer to find researchers interested in, and working on, a subject rather than commission an individual with no demonstrated interest in the area. The main purposes of this paper are to identify major research problems, or topics, which will be significant in the future; indicate the factors which should be considered in approaching these topics to specify the problem and select a research method; and reflect upon the relationships which should be achieved among research, theory, and practice. An underlying purpose of the paper is to interest qualified individuals in conducting research for the AICPA's auditing research program.

The Relation of Practice, Theory, and Research in Auditing

Research is the meeting ground of theory and practice for any applied field of knowledge. In its most general form, the research

---

*Presented at the University of Kansas Symposium on Auditing Problems, Lawrence, Kansas, May 11 and 12, 1972.

[1] See D. R. Carmichael, "The Auditing Research Program," *The Journal of Accountancy*, October 1970, pp. 90-91, for a more complete explanation.

process consists of the identification and measurement of variables that are relevant to a given problem or phenomenon and determination of the nature and strength of the interrelationships among these variables. The research process cannot ignore either theory or practice.

Auditing Theory and Practice. The link between theory and practice, however, exists apart from their intersection in the realm of research. In a treatise on accounting theory, A. C. Littleton offered the following observation on this interrelationship:

> Practice is fact and action; theory consists of explanations and reasons. Theory states the reason why accounting action is what it is, why it is not otherwise, or why it might well be otherwise.[2]

While the need for and desirability of a theory of accounting have been well-accepted for a respectable length of time, the subject of auditing, until recently, has remained for many a completely practical field of knowledge. From the "theory as explanation" viewpoint, there has been a steady development of auditing theory on a piecemeal basis. Examples of this piecemeal development include the recognition of auditing standards and their differentiation from procedures, and explication of the nature and classification of evidential matter.

However, a theory is something more than discrete bits of explanation; theory is comprehensive explanation. A theory of auditing should be an organized and systematized body of knowledge of the field of auditing, which identifies the variables of auditing practice and explains their importance, interrelationships, and implications.

At the close of their treatise on auditing theory, Mautz and Sharaf made the following observation on the interrelationship of theory and practice:

> In the past, auditing has been conceived only as a practical subject with little need for or possibility of any underlying theory. Thus attention has been given to its practical applications to the almost complete exclusion of theoretical considerations. We hope we have indicated the close connection between the theory and practice of auditing, for we are convinced that the only sure solution to practical problems is through the development and use of theory.[3]

Thus Mautz and Sharaf propose a relationship of interdependence for auditing theory and practice. Adequate consideration cannot be given to the practical applications of auditing without regard to the

---

[2]A. C. Littleton, *Structure of Accounting Theory*, American Accounting Association, 1953, p. 132.

[3]R. K. Mautz and Hussein A. Sharaf, *The Philosophy of Auditing*, American Accounting Association, 1961, p. 248.

supporting theory. On the other hand, auditing theory developed to the exclusion of practical considerations cannot fulfill its primary justification for existence.

Mautz and Sharaf characterize the field of auditing knowledge as:

> ... a rigorous field of study able to make a substantial contribution to our economic life and one requiring considerable attention not only to the development of a systematic and satisfactory theory but to the application of such a theory to its practical problems.[4]

Since auditing is an applied field, its ultimate contribution must be made at the practice level. Thus, the ultimate test of auditing theory is its application to the practical problems of auditing.

Auditing Research. The juncture of theory and practice becomes most apparent and important in auditing research. In broad outline, research relies upon practice to identify problems or phenomenon for study, and it relies upon theory to guide the complex task of organizing the facts and actions of practice into a systematic pattern. Without a scheme of organization, the real significance of the collected observations of practice might never surpass the level of description. Without the direction of practice to important problems, the significance of theory might not escape the level of trivia. Thus, research brings theory into contact with practice for the purpose of expanding knowledge and, in the process, research both explains practice and heightens the impact of theory. These, then, are the general relationships of practice, theory, and research.

Research in Auditing

The relationships may be highlighted in more detail by a more intensive examination of research. The research process in its ideal form has been described as follows:

> First, the scientist notes some phenomenon of interest (Y); in the case of social science, Y is some aspect of human behavior. Then he notes variation in the phenomenon: sometimes Y is present, sometimes not; or sometimes Y exists at a high intensity while it has lower intensity at other times. The scientist then begins a search for concomitants (X's) of the phenomenon Y; that is, he tries to discover conditions (X's) under which Y is or is not present, or conditions (X's) which vary as Y varies. When the scientist has identified an X condition that varies with Y, he then needs to establish whether X causes Y, Y causes X, or X and Y both result from some other phenomenon.
>
> While the general procedure can be stated in a fairly simple form, the

---

[4] *Ibid.*, p. 245

research process by which the procedure is carried out is often complicated, requiring elaborate procedures for measuring phenomena (Y's) and associated conditions (X's) and for taking into account the effects of other conditions (Z's).[5]

Although actual research seldom follows this exact chronological sequence, that is the logical sequence of research procedure.

For the moment, let us pass the process by which a particular phenomenon of interest is selected for study, and consider the question of research method—measurement of variables relevant to a phenomenon and determination of their interrelationships. A convenient scheme for classifying research methods distinguishes the methods on the basis of the type of setting within which data may be collected. The following classification scheme is based upon the degree of abstraction of the data collection setting.[6]

I. *Natural Setting*—Data are obtained from real, existing situations of the type to which the results of the study are intended to apply.

    A. *Surveys*—Typically a random sample of a defined population to determine the distribution of a particular characteristic—usually attitudes, opinions, motivations, or expectations of people.

    B. *Field Studies*—Study of a situation which includes the phenomenon of interest to observe and record the phenomenon and its surrounding conditions in detail. This method is well suited for exploratory research to determine major variables. In contrast, the survey is a broader study of selected variables.

    C. *Field Experiments*—A natural setting with some control exercised over selected major variables.

II. *Abstract Setting*—Data are obtained from a setting constructed by the researcher.

    A. *Experimental Simulation*—A created situation which is a relatively faithful representation of the natural setting to study the activities of the participants. Such studies vary greatly in terms of the degree of fidelity to reality.

    B. *Laboratory Experiments*—A setting which abstracts variables from the real situation, represents them in some symbolic

---

[5] Joseph E. McGrath, *Social Psychology*, Holt, Rinehart and Winston, New York, 1964, p. 23.
[6] Adapted from Joseph E. McGrath, "Toward a 'Theory of Method' for Research on Organizations," *New Perspectives in Organization Research*, W. W. Cooper, H. J. Leavitt, and M. W. Shelley, eds., John Wiley & Sons, New York, 1964, pp. 535-540.

form, and studies the operation in that form.

C. *Computer Simulation*—A closed model (mathematical) of the situation studied; all variables are built into the model.

Since each of these methods has some disadvantages in terms of what it cannot do as well as some advantages in terms of what it can do, the methods are not freely interchangeable. The particular research problem should determine the choice of method in any given instance.

Generally, research methods with a natural setting offer less opportunity for control of variables by the researcher than those with an abstract setting. Consequently, in the natural setting, measurement of variables is less precise, and less certainty exists that the research results are attributable to a particular variable. On the other hand, with more abstract settings, gains in precision of measurement and control of variables are accompanied by a loss of realism. Since the settings are abstracted and artificial representations of the real-life conditions under which the phenomena actually occur, more doubt surrounds the applicability of the research results to real-life situations.

More important than considerations of realism versus precision is the extent of prior knowledge about the problem implied by the choice of research setting. To use the more abstract settings, the researcher must either know or assume that he knows a good deal more about the phenomenon of interest than with natural settings. In the abstract setting, the researcher *creates* the situation and must know what conditions need to be controlled. As the research setting becomes more abstract, the research results become more and more a function of the structure imposed by the researcher.

Although the natural settings impose less structure on the situation, this does not mean that no structure at all is imposed. The choice of research setting highlights an important relationship between theory and research. When abstract settings are used, the researcher must incorporate theory in the situation before the data are collected. In contrast, when using natural settings, the researcher collects the data and then incorporates theory as he interprets the data.

Examples of Auditing Research

Some examples of existing auditing research should make the categories distinguished in this classification of methods more meaningful. This review of extant research, for convenience, begins with the more abstract settings. To my knowledge, no computer simulations involving auditing problems have been attempted; the most abstract setting used has been the laboratory experiment.

Behavioral Impact of Audits. Churchill, with the assistance of several others, demonstrated that the performance of the audit function influences the people whose activities are audited. Using laboratory experiments, they have shown that both the anticipation of an audit and the occurrence of an audit cause people to modify their behavior.[7] According to these experiments, audits evidently exert a positive influence on conformance with prescribed control procedures.

To conduct the experiments, Churchill abstracted the key variables in an audit and represented them symbolically in the laboratory. The subjects were given a simple problem-solving task—locating a polluting water station in a water system represented by colored lights in a wired keyboard—and a prescribed method for solving the problem. Some groups were reviewed to see if they complied with the prescribed solution approach, and some groups were told they would be reviewed in advance of their first attempt at solving the problem. By ignoring the prescribed method and innovating, the subjects could solve the problem more efficiently. Thus, the key elements of an audit were present: (1) actions of the participants, (2) prescribed criteria for those actions, and (3) a comparison of the actions and the criteria. Note that in the laboratory experiment no attempt is made to recreate the setting of the real situation under study.

Departure from an APB Opinion. Moving up the continuum to the less abstract experimental simulation, a study by Purdy, Smith, and Gray indicates that implicit assumptions commonly made concerning the effect of reports on users may not be valid.[8] Their experimental simulation tested the visibility of the required notice of departure from an APB Opinion. In October 1964, the Council of the AICPA issued a Special Bulletin stating, in part, that departures from an APB Opinion, if they have "substantial authoritative support," may be disclosed either (1) in the auditor's report or (2) in a footnote to the financial statements, with no qualification of the auditor's opinion. This study measured the visibility of these two alternative methods of disclosure to financial statement users. Contrary to normal expectations, the researchers found that the two forms of disclosure—footnote versus auditor's report—were equally visible to financial statement users.

The research method involved several groups of businessmen

---

[7] Neil C. Churchill and William W. Cooper, "Effects of Auditing Records: Individual Task Accomplishment and Organization Objectives," *New Perspectives in Organization Research*, pp. 250-275; Neil C. Churchill, William W. Cooper, and Trevor Sainsbury, "Laboratory and Field Studies of the Behavioral Effect of Audits," *Management Controls*, Bonini, Jaedicke, and Wagner, eds., McGraw-Hill, Inc., New York, 1964, pp. 253-267.

[8] Charles R. Purdy, Jay M. Smith, and Jack Gray, "The Visibility of the Auditor's Disclosure of Deviance from APB Opinion: An Empirical Test," *Empirical Research in Accounting: Selected Studies 1969.*

familiar with financial statements—such as bankers—who were presented with a set of financial statements accompanied by footnotes and an auditor's report. Some groups received statements disclosing the departure in a footnote, while others received statements disclosing the departure in the audit report. These subjects were then asked questions about the statements.

In contrast to the laboratory experiment, the experimental simulation attempted to achieve some degree of fidelity to reality. Although the participants realized that they were involved in some sort of research study, there was an attempt to approximate the actual analysis of financial statements.

Confirmation of Receivables. Several field experiments have been conducted of the audit procedure of mail confirmation.[9] In all the studies, confirmation requests were sent to actual individuals or businesses. Thus, the setting was natural, and the control exercised by researchers involved only major variables—the form of the confirmation request and the dollar amount of the account balance identified in the request (two studies) or a surrogate for the balance.

Auditee Attitudes. Churchill followed his laboratory studies of the audit process with a field study. Field interviews of people in organizations who had experienced audits (auditees) indicated that they did not perceive the audit as influencing their behavior, and viewed it primarily as a procedural check and somewhat of a policing function.[10] These results are in direct contrast to the laboratory findings that audits did influence behavior.

While the conflicting results of these two studies need not concern us here, their temporal order is of interest. The research began at the abstract setting stage with laboratory experiments. The question I wish to raise is whether auditing researchers should first conduct more extensive studies using a natural setting. In the social sciences, one researcher suggested this ordered progression in the use of research methods:

> If we are starting research on a relatively unexplored phenomenon, it would seem best to start far over at the field study end of the continuum. As

---

[9]Thomas D. Hubbard and Jerry B. Bullington, "Positive and Negative Confirmation Requests—A Test," *The Journal of Accountancy,* March 1972, pp. 48-56; Eugene Sauls, "Nonsampling Errors in Accounts Receivable Confirmation," *The Accounting Review,* January 1972, pp. 109-115; Gordon B. Davis, John Neter, and Roger R. Palmer, "An Experimental Study of Audit Confirmation," *The Journal of Accountancy,* June 1967, pp. 36-44. For an analysis of the import of this type of research see the article review of an earlier study by Sauls in *The Journal of Accountancy,* November 1971, p. 94.
[10]Neil C. Churchill and William W. Cooper, "A Field Study of Internal Auditing," *The Accounting Review,* October 1965, pp. 767-781.

we learn more about the problem, we can then work with methods further along the continuum, with which we can gain more precise information. Then having explored the problem with precision and in depth, and perhaps having formulated and thoroughly manipulated a formal model, we can return toward the field study end of the street to find out how closely our presentations fit the phenomena of the real world.[11]

This suggested order, at least, proved beneficial in the study of criteria used for the different types of auditor's reports described in the next section.

The AICPA's ARM No. 1. The study of the fourth standard of reporting described in *Auditing Research Monograph No. 1* used a natural setting—the field study. The choice of research setting was more or less dictated by the extent of prior knowledge of the reporting decision process. With so little prior knowledge, an explanatory study was needed to identify the important variables. The purpose of the study was to determine the meaning of "sufficiently material"—the single reporting criterion offered in Chapter 10 of SAP No. 33 for distinguishing between qualified opinions and adverse opinions and disclaimers of opinion.

It is interesting to consider how the choice of another method might have influenced the research results. If an abstract setting, such as an experimental simulation or a laboratory experiment, had been chosen, certain assumptions would have been necessary in the design of the study. If "sufficiently material" had been equated with relative magnitude, that variable would have been manipulated by varying the dollar impact of the exception. Research results would have established relative magnitude cut-off points for distinguishing between "material" and "sufficiently material" based on reporting decisions made by the subjects. Note the extent to which the research results would have been influenced by the structure imposed on the setting. On the other hand, research results obtained by a case-by-case study of audit reports indicate that certain qualitative variables seem to be more important than, or at least as important as, the quantitative variable.

Surveys. Recently, there has been a virtual explosion of surveys dealing with auditing topics. In fact they are too numerous to identify specifically, and singling out any one study for attention is not essential since most accountants are by now quite familiar with this type of research. However, far too many of the current surveys deal with insignificant problems and, in my view, the survey method of research is being abused today. This observation naturally leads to the critical

---

[11]McGrath, "Toward a Theory of Method," p. 555.

question: What are the significant problems which should attract the attention of auditing researchers?

Recommendations for Future Research

Developments in auditing research, theory, and practice are by nature evolutionary. For example, the research reported in ARM No. 1 should serve as a foundation, or at least provide a background, for future study of the decision-making process of auditors in reporting. ARM No. 1 identifies the central reporting concepts and describes the role of these concepts in reporting decisions. With limited prior knowledge about the subject, the research method sacrificed some precision and several questions remain to be answered. Care was taken to obtain the data from real, existing situations of the type to which the results were intended to apply. This constraint need not be applied so stringently in future studies, and precision of measurement may be increased by using more abstract methods—with one or two important reporting concepts isolated for study. This approach makes possible exploration of phenomena which do not occur frequently in practice, such as situations leading to adverse opinions. However, the reporting decision process is certainly not the only important research topic. Many other subjects are important, some of which are outlined below.

A. Expansion of the Attest Function

1. Historical Financial Summaries. (What are the minimum requirements for fair presentation?)

2. Interim Financial Statements. (What evidential matter is necessary to support an opinion, and can the evidence gathering process be structured to implement the continuous auditing concept?)

3. Forecasts or Projected Financial Statements. (What degree of responsibility for assumptions should the CPA assume in light of the nature of evidence available and the comprehension capabilities of the report reader?)

4. Operational Auditing. (What type of audit report is appropriate, and what form of evidential matter is adequate to support the report when propriety criteria are not well formulated?)

B. Refinement of Auditing Methods

1. Use of Other Experts. (In what circumstances should evidential matter include the work of other experts—such as

geologists, actuaries, lawyers, or engineers—and should any reference be made to these experts in the audit report?)

2. Auditing Fair Value. (What forms of evidential matter are necessary to support an opinion on financial information based upon fair value rather than historical cost?)

C. Professional Responsibilities

1. Objectivity and Integrity. (What alternative arrangements for selecting, changing, and compensating auditors would be feasible?)

2. Communication Responsibility. (To whom—both within the audited entity and outside the entity—and in what manner should the auditor communicate knowledge which may fall outside the audit report on financial statements, such as illegal acts, internal control weaknesses, and improper client-prepared financial information?)

These are the auditing subjects which I would regard as most significant for future study. Each topic is followed by the major question to be answered, which would have to be reduced to a number of relevant researchable questions. This distinction is very important—in fact, critical. Each problem must be specified in terms of more specific researchable questions so that evidence and information may be gathered that bear directly on the problem. Mautz and Gray expressed the point in this way:

> The specific issue must be stated in such a way that it meets the needs for which the research is proposed and indicates the kind of evidence relevant to the research subject. The research methodology must be such that it will provide convincing evidence and valid reasoning from that evidence. [12]

The Mautz and Gray article is such a well-reasoned blueprint for effective research that expanding greatly upon what they have said so well is not necessary. In the auditing research program, we have endeavored to follow a similar approach from the very beginning of the formal program.

Problem specification is such an important aspect of research that I would like to explore—as an illustration—some of the factors considered in the preparation of ARM No. 1. Many, if not most, discussions of research method focus on the steps in the process after the phenomenon of interest has been selected for study and the problem specified in some detail. However, problem selection and

---

[12] R. K. Mautz and Jack Gray, "Some Thoughts on Research Needs in Accounting," *The Journal of Accountancy*, September 1970, p. 58.

specification are critical steps in the research process. It is at this point that research should draw significantly upon practice. The difficult problems in practice, at the profession level, should identify what phenomena require study and explication. Determination of the important questions to be answered—specification of the problem—should also rely heavily on practice. An exploratory review of practice to determine the major questions to be answered should be undertaken in every study, no matter what research setting is chosen to collect data.

In the study of the fourth reporting standard reported in ARM No. 1, an initial study of practice disclosed that the primary problem was lack of criteria for the distinction between a "subject to" qualification and a disclaimer of opinion. Consequently, uncertainty exceptions received the bulk of attention in the study. Further exploration disclosed that one particular type of uncertainty exception—the going-concern problem—was of major importance and, therefore, that subject was given more extensive treatment than other types of uncertainties.

For a number of reasons, research directed to the influence of audit reports in the decision process of financial statement users did not seem appropriate for an initial study. Although future research should definitely consider this dimension of the reporting process, careful attention should be given to those factors that eliminated that approach as an initial choice.

To study the decision process of financial statement users and retain control over the relevant variables, an experimental simulation or a laboratory experiment would seem to be the most logical choice for a data-collection setting. The problems involved in this research approach can be conveniently explored by considering one possible experiment. If we want to test the users' reaction to different types of audit reports when a material uncertainty is present, we might prepare a set of financial statements for a company that has a large amount of research and development cost of doubtful recoverability with extensive footnote disclosure of the problem. Different groups would be presented with the financial statements and accompanying auditor's report, and control would be exercised over the type of report. One group would receive statements with a qualified opinion; another group would receive the same statements with a disclaimer of opinion; and the statements received by a third group would be accompanied by an unqualified opinion. Other sets of financial statements would be used to vary the relative magnitude of the amount involved. In this manner, the impact of the type of audit report on users could be measured. However, while establishing the data stimuli is not too difficult, the method of measuring response is more troublesome.

An easy approach would be to allow the subjects to read through the information and then, without allowing reference to the statements, have them answer a series of questions about the statements. In this fashion, it would be possible to determine whether variations in the audit report created a greater awareness of the uncertainty problem. However, this approach does not get at the critical question of whether the audit report has an impact on the decision process of the user. Would variations in the audit report cause any change in the user's decision? Would the different decisions be better decisions?

Research on the impact of the audit report on the decision process adds an extremely complex element to an already difficult research problem. Research of this sort would require some knowledge of the financial statement user's forecasting model—conversion of historical data into estimates of the future—and his decision model—interaction of the estimates—in reaching a decision. Research on the decision process typically assumes that all data presented to the subjects is of equal reliability. The subject is given no reason to doubt the veracity of the data. Introducing degrees of qualification concerning the reliability of the data considerably complicates the research problem.

Usually in research of this type, to achieve adequate controls over the experimental situation, the phenomenon of interest must be simplified to such an extent that only a portion of the phenomenon can be captured, and the research results are of doubtful applicability to the "real world" situation abstracted in the experiment. Consequently, the potential results of this type of research did not hold enough promise to serve as a basis for major policy decisions. In addition, with so little information available on the decision process of auditors, establishing the criteria actually used by auditors seemed to be a more logical starting point. Future research, however, should begin to delve into this complex aspect of the reporting process.

Those of us involved in the auditing research effort at the AICPA hope that the above list will serve as an early identification of significant research topics and stimulate the interest of academic researchers capable of performing adequate research on the issues.

Research Environment

Those performing research, however, should recognize that a distinction exists between academic and, for want of a better word, institutional research—meaning research conducted for a professional organization. Naturally, we expect the two to be different, but while some of the differences are legitimate, others are of doubtful merit and might well be eliminated.

Time-Span. Generally, academic research may be conducted over a longer time-span. Time constraints are usually personal and imposed by the desire or interest of the researcher. An academic researcher may envision a series of related studies conducted over a long period of time with each new study making additional refinements to the previous effort. Institutional research must usually go directly from research results to implementing guidelines for practice. The study is usually related to the development of a professional pronouncement or a firm position, and pressing deadlines may be attached to these publications.

Real-World Referents. Academic research frequently opts for the simplification and control of highly abstract research settings. Experiments and simulations allow precise measurement of variables, which is attractive even though there may be some doubt about the applicability of the results to the "real world." On the other hand, institutional research must often accept the loss of rigor and control to gain greater confidence that the research results are applicable to practice.

Audience. Academic research is in many cases unabashedly aimed at other academicians, while institutional research must satisfy policymakers and practitioners as well as other researchers. Since these groups undoubtedly have different norms and values, the reaction to institutional research results is likely to be mixed.

Subject Choice. Institutional research almost always begins with a problem to be solved. Little opportunity exists for restricting and tailoring the problem; the research method must be fitted to the problem so that it may be answered by the available evidence. If the problem is defined and narrowed too much, the institutional researcher will fall far short of his task. In contrast, academic researchers in many cases seem to choose a research method they would like to employ and then search for a problem that might be solved by that method.

Bureaucratic Infringement. Institutional research seems to be obviously plagued by possible conflicts between bureaucratic and professional norms. However, the academic researcher has a similar problem. In fact, his plight may be greater because the problem is much harder to recognize. The university is a complex organization, and survival and advancement in the academic community at times requires compliance with norms that may be in conflict with the ideals of a scholar. Blind adherence to an in-vogue research method may take precedence over generation of fresh insight on difficult problems. The nonparametric test of significance may assume more importance than the actual significance—that is, the relevance and importance—of the research results to the resolution of any real problem. As a consequence, too often academic research results in a glorification of technicians over discoverers, quantification for its own sake, and fitting problems to research techniques rather than the reverse.

Concluding Remarks

Auditing theory is important, but theory developed in isolation from the problems of practice at the profession level has little significance and risks being trivial. Note that there is a substantial difference between those problems which face the auditing profession collectively and those problems raised in each individual audit.

To be worthwhile in the effort of solving significant problems, auditing research must be empirical. Deductive reasoning and attention to theory may never be ignored, and these elements should play an instrumental part in any auditing research. A clear specification of the problem, which is primarily a process of logic, may be the most important step in the research process. However, a convincing solution to an important problem is not likely without empirical evidence on the issues.

There are many forms of empirical research. Too often empirical research in accounting has meant research methods employing an abstract data collection setting, with the possible exception of the ubiquitous "survey." At this stage in the development of the auditing field of knowledge, there is probably a greater need for field studies and field experiments, or, at least, a combination of these methods with the more abstract methods in an ordered program of research.

In closing, while I would not discourage any kind of auditing research, I would encourage research directed to the problems identified in this paper that gives full recognition to the role of practice, as well as theory, in the research process. There is no legitimate distinction between theoretical and applied research in auditing since neither theory nor practice can reach its full potential with the exclusion of the other.